LIVING Our FAITH
God
Revelation and Relationship

Principal **Consultants**

Dennis J. Bozanich, MBA

Michael Carotta, EdD

Rev. Leonard Wenke, MDiv

Principal **Reviewers**

Mary Lee Becker, MPM

Robert J. Kealey, EdD

M. Annette Mandley-Turner, MS

Harcourt
Religion Publishers

Nihil Obstat
Rev. Richard L. Schaefer
Censor Deputatus

Imprimatur
✠ Most Rev. Jerome Hanus, OSB
Archbishop of Dubuque
January 31, 2001
Feast of Saint John Bosco, Patron of Youth and Catholic Publishers

The nihil obstat and imprimatur are official declarations that a book or pamphlet is free of doctrinal or moral error. No implication is contained herein that those who granted the nihil obstat and imprimatur agree with the contents, opinions, or statements expressed.

Our Mission
The primary mission of Harcourt Religion Publishers is to provide the Catholic and Christian educational markets with the highest quality catechetical print and media resources. The content of these resources reflects the best insights of current theology, methodology, and pedagogical research. These resources are practical and easy to use, designed to meet expressed market needs, and written to reflect the teachings of the Catholic Church.

Photography Credits
AP Wide World Photos: Arturo Mari: 6; **Bridge Buildings Images:** Burlington, VT: Jesus of the People © 1999/Janet McKenzie 55; **Bridgeman Art Library:** Baptistery, Florence, Italy: 59; **Cleo Photography:** 12; **Convent Franciscans of Marytown:** Libertyville, IL: 47; **Corbis:** 74, 79; **The Croisers:** Gene Plaisted: 37, 55, 56, 57, 67, 70, 78, 87, 88; **Digital Imaging Group:** Erik Snowbeck: 32; **Foundation Teilhard de Chardin:** 17; **FPG International:** Ken Chernus: 48; David Micheal Davis: 36; Rob Gage: 38; Barry Rosenthal: 49; Telegraph Colour Library: 11; **Jack Holtel:** 14, 32, 34, 44, 45, 61, 64, 81, 94; **Image Bank:** David W. Hamilton: 6; Yellow Dog Prods: 16; **International Christian Concern**/www.persecution.org: 19; **Jesuit Volunteer Corps:** Amy C. Postel: 98; **Natural Bridges:** Robert Lentz Collection: 67; **Nicholas Studios:** Nick Falzerano: 86, 96, 97; **PhotoEdit:** Deborah Davis: 29; Myrleen Ferguson Cate: 27, 62, 85; Micheal Newman: 66; David Young-Wolff: 99, 103; **Photo Researchers:** Michael Austin: 21; Richard Hutchings: 58; **Picture Quest:** Chris Niedenthal/Black Star Publishing: 7; **David Sanger Photography:** Artist Mark Dukes: 37; **Stock Boston:** Bob Daemmrich: 9, 98; Stephen Frisch: 29; S. S. Groet: 16; Kent Knudson: 84; Paul Mozell: 68; Frank Siteman: 29; **The Stock Market:** Charles Gupton: 8; Jose L. Pelaez: 17; **Stone:** Robert Freck: 57; Walter Hodges: 19; Andy Sacks: 26; David Stewart: 72; David Young-Wolff: 40, 100; **Superstock:** 7, 21, 22, 25, 27, 31, 43, 46, 48, 77; American Bible Society, New York: 18; Armenian Museum, Venice: 24; Musee du Louvre, Paris: 37; **Trip Photo Library:** H. Rogers: 74; **Unicorn Stock:** Florant Flipper: 7; **Jim Whitmer Photography:** Jim Whitmer: 4, 38, 52, 69, 76, 79, 83, 89, 91

Cover Photos
FPG International: Telegraph Colour Library; Jack Holtel

Feature Icons
Catholics Believe: Jack Holtel; **Opening the Word:** PictureQuest; **Our Christian Journey:** PictureQuest: Chuck Fishman/Contact Press Images

Location and Props
Dayton Church Supply; St. Christopher Catholic School, Vandalia, OH; St. Peter Catholic School, Huber Heights, OH

Skills for Christian Living
The skill steps in Recognizing God's Presence and How to Pray, and the Name It, Tame It, Claim It process, all from the *Catholic and Capable* series, are used with permission from Resources for Christian Living.

Printed in the United States of America

ISBN 0-15-900488-8
10 9 8 7 6 5 4 3 2 1

LIVING Our FAITH
God
Revelation and Relationship

Search for God

Loving God, we seek to know you better. Your goodness is beyond our understanding; your love is more vast than we can ever know. Guide us in your ways.

What Do You Think?

On the clock faces below, mark the times when you are most likely to turn to or think about God.

Explain why you chose the above times.

_____

_____

_____

Written in the
Human Heart

Humans have a deep inner desire to experience the divine. From primitive societies to complex industrial civilizations, most cultures have formed a religious belief system that indicates a quest for God.

In our lifetime we search for God in many different ways—from joining in the liturgy with our Church community to appreciating God's gift of a person who loves us. The more open we become to God's presence, the more we can experience him in our everyday lives. We can begin to see him in a sunrise or in our baby brother's smile.

Recent studies have shown that the more we allow ourselves to experience God, the happier and healthier we will be. Why do you think that is? A big part of the reason is because when we recognize and celebrate God's presence, we are overjoyed and we want to share our experience of his love with those around us. We worry and argue less, and we share our talents more. God both creates us and sustains us.

The Limitations of **Experience**

Think of a school musical production. There are many people involved with the presentation of the play, and many other people come to watch the play. Even though only one play is being performed, there will be many different experiences of the event. The students in charge of lighting the stage will be focused on specific lines of dialogue or gestures as cues to turn lights on or off. The actors performing in the play might remember only the scenes in which they took part. Members of the audience will see the entire play from start to finish, but they will have no knowledge of what is going on backstage or down in the orchestra pit.

In much the same way, the human mind is too limited to grasp God entirely. We have pieced together various truths about our Creator, and yet the entire reality of God is beyond what we have been able to fully understand and express. With reason and faith, we can come to know God, who reveals himself to us.

Naming the **Divine**

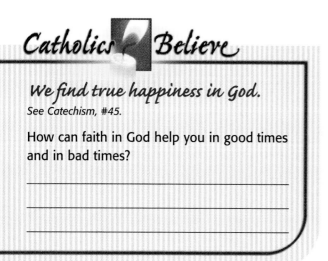

Catholics Believe

We find true happiness in God.
See Catechism, #45.

How can faith in God help you in good times and in bad times?

_____

_____

_____

A **religion** is a system of beliefs and practices that express a group's faith in God. This belief structure influences the way we live in relationship to others. It is fascinating to compare the names that different religions use for God and to learn what people have believed about the nature of God.

According to the Islamic religion, all things came into existence when *Allāh,* the creator, spoke the word *Be.* Islam assigns seven attributes to the nature of Allāh: Life, Knowledge, Power, Will, Hearing, Sight, and Speech.

Allāh's major prophet was a man named Muhammad, who revealed the Ninety-Nine Beautiful Names of Allāh. The first of these is *al-Rahmán,* which is translated as "The Compassionate." Other Islamic names for God

Bringing Churches Together The ecumenical movement is a worldwide effort to increase cooperation between Churches. This process began among Protestant Churches at a World Missionary Conference in Edinburgh, Scotland, in 1910. For the first few decades, this movement was almost entirely a Protestant effort.

At that time the Catholic Church resisted this movement, but in 1961 Pope John XXIII sent official observers to the third assembly of the World Council of Churches.

Then in 1964 the Catholic bishops approved a decree called *The Restoration of Unity,* calling all Catholics to support the cause of Christian unity. The document states that grace fosters unity among all Christians. The ecumenical movement is at its beginning stages and has as its hope and goal the unity of all Christians in the one and only Church of Christ.

For further information: Research other councils or movements that seek to unite Christians. Is there any common bond among these types of groups or movements?

1925   1975

1926
FORMATION OF THE COMMONWEALTH OF NATIONS

1945
FORMATION OF THE UNITED NATIONS

1948
FORMATION OF THE WORLD COUNCIL OF CHURCHES

1964
THE RESTORATION OF UNITY APPROVED

include: The Peace, The Generous, The Gatherer, The Powerful, The Mighty, and The Forgiver.

Members of the Hindu religion believe in the existence of more than one god. The three major divinities within Hinduism are *Brahma,* the creator God; *Vishnu,* the protector of the world and of spirituality; and *Shiva,* the destroyer who makes room for a new universe. Hindus believe in a unity behind all reality and seek enlightenment through various forms of meditation.

The Buddhist religion is based on a "Middle Path," or balance, in all areas of life rather than on a belief in God. Its "Way of Life" comes from the teachings of Siddhartha Gautama (c. 563–c. 483 B.C.). The name *Buddha* means "Awakened One" or "Enlightened One" and can be applied to anyone who has reached a state of enlightenment, or spiritual awakening, called *Nirvana.* Buddhist values include mercy, nonviolence, and the suppression of passions and desires, such as gaining possessions or searching for someone to marry.

In Judaism the name of God, YHWH, which is considered sacred, was revealed to Moses. This name has been translated both as "I am who am" and "He who is." Prior to the destruction of the temple in A.D. 70, the name of God was spoken only once a year by the high priest in the innermost room of the temple, known as the Holy of Holies.

There are many religions, which are all trying to grasp the same reality—God. From the many religious experiences, God draws people to himself.

With your Faith Partner, design and complete a chart that highlights important aspects of each of the religions mentioned above. Then add Christianity to your chart.

opening the Word

For it was you who formed my inward parts;
you knit me together in my mother's womb.
I praise you, for I am fearfully and wonderfully made.
Wonderful are your works;
that I know very well. Psalm 139:13–14

Read *Psalm 139:1–18* and *Sirach 42:15–25*. Why is God so awe-inspiring?

_____

_____

_____

_____

Beyond Belief

Faith is a gift from God. This gift moves us to search for him and believe in him. But we need God's help in our faith-seeking. Through his guidance and with the help of the Holy Spirit, we can learn about God and our relationship with him. For Christians faith includes a belief in the Father, Son, and Holy Spirit. Faith is the beginning of eternal life.

As we grow in our faith, we ask questions. Who is God? Why do I believe in God? These questions are natural. Because having faith means trusting God's word, we look for answers in his revelation. We read Scripture, we observe his creation, and we experience him through the good works of people around us. Through our faith in him and in his plan, we are able to answer many of the questions we have. As

Paul says in his first Letter to the Corinthians, we are guided by our faith, not by our sight. (See *2 Corinthians 5:7.*) In other words, we can never hope to explain God through human knowledge alone. God is more than any of those things. We know God because we have faith in God.

From our faith in God, we develop the beliefs and values by which we live our lives. A *belief* is something we hold to be true. For instance, when we were babies, we believed the world revolved around us. We didn't take into account anyone's feelings but our own, nor did we think we needed to. All we needed to do was eat, sleep, and experience the love of our family. As we grew older, our world expanded. We met friends from our neighborhood or school. We began to believe that to take part in these relationships, it was important to share— share time, share attention, and share the things we had. Now as we have grown older, these relationships have become more complex. We now believe that to be a true friend, we need to be kind, considerate, and welcoming. In the process of developing our friendships, we have incorporated our faith into our belief.

Like our beliefs, our values develop out of our faith. A *value* is an attitude or idea about which we feel very strongly. It is a principle upon which we base our decisions. Within Christianity our values are based on our faith. If we value the dignity of every person, our attitude will be one of compassion and forgiveness. In turn we will act in a way that reflects Christian values and attitudes.

Ultimately, faith is lived. We believe certain things and we value certain qualities. But only when we put our faith into action do we express what we believe and what we value. The more we experience God, the more we learn his plan for us. As we better understand his plan, we allow his love and guidance into our lives and we begin to share it with others.

Media Message

SAY IT WITH BUMPER STICKERS One of the most enduring fads to come out of the 1960s is the bumper sticker. These stickers were first used for political slogans during presidential campaigning. Over the years the number of topics increased, covering every subject from handgun control to making the honor roll. Some bumper stickers have a religious message, with one of the more famous being the "Honk if you love Jesus" sticker that was popular in the early 1970s.

What bumper sticker have you seen that made you think about God in a new way? In the space below, create your own bumper sticker that says something unique about your experience of God.

Our Experience of God

We experience the world through our five senses: sight, hearing, touch, smell, and taste. But this is not how we experience God. So how are we supposed to experience and learn about God?

Because of our faith heritage, we believe that humans are created in the image and likeness of God. This means that God is reflected in all of us. So one very strong way of experiencing God in our lives is through our relationships with the people in our lives.

In *1 John 4:12* the statement is made that no one has ever seen God. But the author further explains that if we love one another, God lives in us and his love is brought to perfection in us. Experiencing God becomes a matter of loving one another.

Reflect on your own experience of God. Who or what helps you learn about God in your life? Share your thoughts with your Faith Partner.

FaiTH PaRTNeRSHiP

WRAP UP

- Humans have a deep desire to experience God in their lives.
- There are many religions, all seeking the same knowledge—God.
- Faith is the gift from God that causes us to search for him and to believe in him.
- We can experience God most through loving others.

What questions do you have about the information presented in this chapter?

_____

_____

_____

Around the Group

Discuss the following question as a group.

What do you think is the most effective way to learn about God?

After everyone has had a chance to share his or her most effective method, come up with a group answer upon which everyone can agree.

_____

_____

_____

_____

What personal observations do you have about the group discussion and answer?

_____

_____

_____

_____

Briefly...

At the beginning of this chapter, you reflected on when you think about God. Now, based upon what you have learned, list some questions you have concerning God.

_____

_____

_____

Recognizing God's Presence

Expressions of Faith—

Recognizing God's presence is not always easy, because God tends to "whisper" when he communicates his love to us. We live in a world full of so much noise and busyness that it can be difficult to hear God. Part of the skill of Recognizing God's Presence involves filtering out the "noise" in our lives that prevents us from listening to the gentle voice of God.

Scripture

God is love, and those who abide in love abide in God, and God abides in them.

1 John 4:16 7th Sunday of Easter, Cycle B

Think About It—

List three to five things, or "noises," that make it hard to recognize God's voice.

_____

_____

_____

_____

_____

_____

_____

_____

_____

Skill Steps-

Believing in God and knowing about God are not the same as recognizing God's presence.

We experience God not only in other humans but also in the physical world. God is revealed to us in love, beauty, and truth.

● Name a truth you've come to realize in regard to creation.

_____

_____

_____

● List two of the most beautiful places you have ever seen.

_____

_____

● Describe a loving act you have witnessed.

_____

_____

_____

Check It Out-

Place a check mark next to the sentences that apply to you.

◯ I recognize God's presence daily.

◯ I've had at least one strong experience of God's presence in my life.

◯ I sometimes am aware of God's presence through my friends.

◯ I find it easy to detect God's presence in nature.

◯ I see beauty in the world around me.

Based on your responses, how would you describe the way you recognize God's presence?

_____

_____

_____

Closing Prayer-

God of Truth, Beauty, and Love, help us recognize your presense in the world around us. Speak to us in your gentle voice, and keep us wrapped in your love.

Loving Creator, you are known to us through your works of creation. Reveal yourself to us in new ways, and help us find you in our daily lives.

How Do We Know God?

What Do You Think?

From earliest childhood we form images of God. These images are influenced by family tradition, the media, your religious education, and even your friends. Examine the words below, and circle each word that corresponds with your image of God.

Teacher	Friend	Judge	Nurturer
Enforcer	Savior	Forgiver	Father
Creator	Ruler	Guardian	Governor
Gatherer	Guide	Lover	Mother

How does your image of God differ from what it was three years ago? As a small child?

_____

_____

_____

_____

Our Design

Imagine riding a tandem bicycle by yourself. What would people think, seeing a bicycle built for two being pedaled by a single rider? How would you feel, having to pedal such a heavy vehicle without the assistance of another person?

While a tandem bike can certainly be ridden solo, it is not designed for that. Its design calls for two riders, and the bicycle will not perform well with only one rider.

Humans, likewise, were created to live and act in a certain way. God created us with a yearning for freedom, for fulfillment, for a sense of completion. We are created for relationship with God.

Finding God in Creation

Revelation is the process by which God makes himself known to us. Creation itself is a source of revelation. So is human history. Scripture is another source of revelation, and Jesus himself is the fullness of God's revelation.

The Book of Genesis contains two creation stories. The first story tells of God creating the world in six days and then resting on the seventh. (See *Genesis 1:1—2:3.*) Catholic biblical scholars do not interpret this story literally, but rather look to the meaning or religious truth in it.

In this creation story we are told that God looked at everything he'd made, and that he found it to be very good. (See *Genesis 1:31.*) The goodness of creation is an important point in this story, because the goodness of creation helps us become aware of the nature of the Creator.

The second creation story represents God almost as an artist, breathing life into humans and fashioning all other living creatures. (See *Genesis 2:4–25.*)

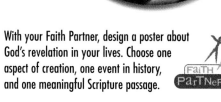

With your Faith Partner, design a poster about God's revelation in your lives. Choose one aspect of creation, one event in history, and one meaningful Scripture passage.

Catholics Believe

We can discover God by examining our human nature, especially our openness to truth and beauty, our sense of moral goodness, and our freedom and conscience. See Catechism, #33.

What does this statement tell us about how we are created?

_____

_____

_____

When we observe creation, we discover marvelous structure and order. Through science we have learned a great deal about the physical laws, such as gravity, that govern the order of creation. We also learn that not everything follows a strict order. For example, within human nature there is freedom.

Humans have the ability to choose. This ability, called *free will,* gives us the opportunity to be creative, to establish our own identities, to take responsibility for our own lives, and to love or not love.

A star, such as the sun, does not have free will. Stars predictably go through stages in which they give off energy in the form of radiation. By studying this process, astrophysicists can determine the age of a given star and predict where it is in its life cycle.

Even though the interior temperature of a star can reach one million degrees Celsius, a human actually has a far greater "power"—the freedom to choose. For instance, we can change our minds about everything from careers to favorite types of music. We can choose to be a loving person, or we can choose to be cruel and selfish. A star does not have this freedom; its destiny and its process never change.

We can use our free will to choose to accomplish wonderful things, and by doing so, have a share in the life of our Creator. In fact, we have a responsibility to use our free will to do good, moral actions rather than evil. We have a responsibility to help

a friend through a difficult time rather than avoiding him or her just because of the time it would take to help. And we gain more responsibility as we mature. We have more freedom to spend time with friends, but we also have the responsibility to choose good friends and healthy activities that do not risk our safety or the safety of others.

OUR CHRISTIAN JOURNEY

Seeing God in Creation Pierre Teilhard de Chardin was born in Auvergne, France. He loved and studied science, especially geology and paleontology. Teilhard de Chardin was involved in

expeditions in China and eventually was given the Legion of Honour for academics.

Teilhard de Chardin sought to reconcile the fields of religion and science. He looked at religious doctrine from a scientific perspective and viewed science with a contemplative, religious eye. One of his main theories was that the material world of rocks and trees, stars and planets, plants and animals could be seen as a mirror reflecting back the face of God.

For further information: Investigate nature in your local area. Observe and research aspects that interest you and then journal your findings.

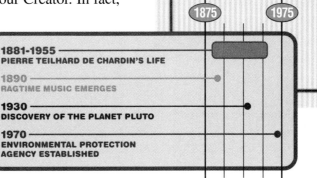

1875   1975

1881-1955 ——
PIERRE TEILHARD DE CHARDIN'S LIFE

1890 ——
RAGTIME MUSIC EMERGES

1930 ——
DISCOVERY OF THE PLANET PLUTO

1970 ——
ENVIRONMENTAL PROTECTION
AGENCY ESTABLISHED

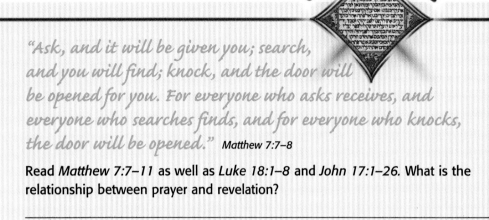

"Ask, and it will be given you; search, and you will find; knock, and the door will be opened for you. For everyone who asks receives, and everyone who searches finds, and for everyone who knocks, the door will be opened." Matthew 7:7–8

Read *Matthew 7:7–11* as well as *Luke 18:1–8* and *John 17:1–26.* What is the relationship between prayer and revelation?

_____

_____

_____

Finding God in History

God chose to reveal himself to humans gradually throughout history and to enable them to share in his divine life. Events leading to this end are related to each other. One event helps us understand another. This process of revelation culminated in the mission of Jesus Christ.

Salvation history is the story of God's loving actions on behalf of humans. It began with creation, continues through the events recorded in Scripture, and will last until the end of time. Salvation history includes more than just religious events. Because God can be known both through creation and through human history, the whole history of the world—geological processes to human accomplishments—are ingredients of salvation history.

Another element of revelation is the story of salvation history in the Old and New Testament Scriptures. These texts were written by humans with the **inspiration,** or guidance, of the Holy Spirit. This knowledge handed down to the Church guides us all in our search for God.

Finding God in **Ourselves**

God also reveals himself in our conscience, our personal sense of moral responsibility. Through our conscience and with the guidance of the Holy Spirit, we realize the importance of acting beyond self-interest alone, acting with the good of others in mind. With God's grace we find ourselves living in harmony with God's creation—using natural resources wisely, treating others with respect, working to promote good policy and the common good in our communities.

God also reveals himself through other people, for we are all created in the image and likeness of God. We get a glimpse of God's love for us, which says a lot about who God is. We can understand something about an artist by reflecting on his or her art. The same applies to God.

With your Faith Partner, discuss how or when people have experienced God through you.

FaiTH PaRTNeRSHiP

Our Global Community

The Underground Church

At various times and in various places during the first three centuries of Christianity, Christians suffered persecution, especially at the hands of the Roman government. In those days many Christians were martyred for their faith and buried in the catacombs, or underground caverns with niches carved into the walls.

Other forms of political persecution continue even today. In August 1999 in the Henan province of China, eight leaders of the "Underground Church" were arrested and sentenced to labor camps. After their houses were ransacked and their Bibles confiscated, family members were told by the police that the leaders had been imprisoned for participating in illegal gatherings. Christians in China often meet for worship in "house churches," and their secret meetings are occasionally disbanded by the police.

Other places where Christians recently have been imprisoned for their faith include Iran, Sudan, and Indonesia.

Making a Difference

The most important question that you, a person of faith, can ask yourself is "What difference does it make whether God is in my life?"

James 2:14–17 deals with the issue of professing faith without practicing it. The author points out that faith without good works is lifeless.

Faith does make a difference. If you are a member of a team and have a strong desire to win, you are attentive and involved in practice sessions, abide by team rules, act on directions, and make teamwork a priority. On the other hand, if you are late for practice, ignore the rules, do not follow directions, and do nothing to improve the performance of the team, the rest of the team could rightly question your faith in the team. So it is with life. Our actions give witness to our faith.

Reflect on your reasons for your belief in God and how that belief affects your life. Share your thoughts with your Faith Partner.

FaiTH PaRTNeRSHiP

WRAP UP

- **Revelation is the process by which God makes himself known to us.**

- **God reveals himself in creation.**

- **God also reveals himself through his actions in salvation history, through Scripture, and fully in Jesus.**

- **Salvation history is the story of God's loving action on behalf of humans.**

What questions do you have about the information presented in this chapter?

_____

_____

_____

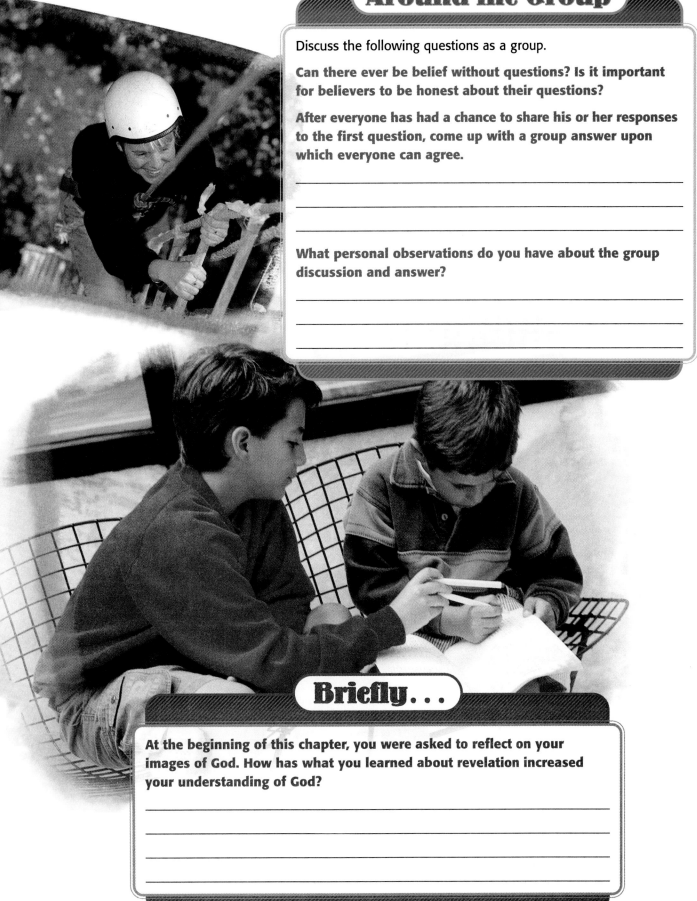

Around the Group

Discuss the following questions as a group.

Can there ever be belief without questions? Is it important for believers to be honest about their questions?

After everyone has had a chance to share his or her responses to the first question, come up with a group answer upon which everyone can agree.

_____

_____

_____

What personal observations do you have about the group discussion and answer?

_____

_____

_____

Briefly...

At the beginning of this chapter, you were asked to reflect on your images of God. How has what you learned about revelation increased your understanding of God?

_____

_____

_____

_____

Recognizing God's Presence

Expressions of Faith—

The more an individual can have faith in God's presence through truth, beauty, and love, the easier it becomes to discover God in everyday life and to rely on God in hardship or sadness.

Skill Steps—

In the first chapter you learned how to recognize God's presence in the truth, beauty, and love that you witnessed around you in nature, in relationships, and in actions. But God is always present in our lives, including those times that we might feel alone or overwhelmed and when we might not believe that there is truth, beauty, or love around us.

Here are some key points to remember:

- There is a difference between believing in God, knowing about God, and actually recognizing God's presence.

- All of us were created in God's image. We naturally long for God's presence.

- The Church has always taught that you can develop the skill of Recognizing God's Presence by looking within truth, beauty, and love, as found in all of creation and especially within the human person.

- You can also recognize the presence of God and the need for God's presence during the absence of truth, beauty, and love.

Scripture

"But ask the animals, and they will teach you;
the birds of the air, and they will tell you;
ask the plants of the earth, and they will teach you;
and the fish of the sea will declare to you.
Who among all these does not know
that the hand of the Lord has done this?
In his hand is the life of every living thing
and the breath of every human being."

Job 12:7–10

Skill Builder-

The flip side of recognizing God's presence in truth, beauty, and love is to recognize God's presence when these three elements are missing. In the lines provided, use a symbol, a word, or an initial to indicate your experience of these instances.

○ A time when you were or someone you know was hurt by a lie

_____

_____

○ A time when you saw something of beauty destroyed

_____

_____

○ A time when you witnessed an unloving act

_____

_____

How or when have any of these experiences been times when you recognized God's presence? Share your responses and thoughts with your Faith Partner.

Putting It into Practice-

Think of a time recently when you recognized God's presence in a situation involving truth, beauty, or love. Compose a prayer of thanksgiving about that time.

_____

_____

_____

Saint Augustine issued this challenge:

> *Question the beauty of the earth, question the beauty of the sea . . . question the beauty of the sky . . . question all these realities. All respond: "See, we are beautiful." . . . Who made them if not the Beautiful One?*

When you question the existence of God, what gives you the best answer: truth, beauty, or love? What are other signs of God's presence for you?

_____

_____

Closing Prayer-

Gentle God, help us see you in the truth, beauty, and love around us. Thank you for revealing yourself to us; continue to show us your ways.

CHAPTER

3

Glorious God, we stand in awe of the universe you created. Help us understand our role within creation, and help us reflect your glory as we go about our lives.

The Glory of God

Stardust

Astronomers tell us the atomic elements that make up the molecules that form our bodies were originally part of some ancient star. We are, quite literally, made from stardust. But where did all that dust originate? How did the elements come into being? One theory is that our universe began with a cosmic explosion called the "big bang," but that still doesn't explain where the material that exploded came from.

Our creed tells us that God is the maker of all things, seen and unseen. At the time of the Council of Nicaea, in A.D. 325, when they spoke about the "unseen," they were referring to phenomena such as angels. Today when scientists talk about the "unseen," they are more likely to think of protons, neutrons, or other subatomic particles. But the fact is, everything spiritual and physical—from angels to protons—comes from God.

Opening the Word

5th Sunday of Ordinary Time, Cycle A

"You are the light of the world. A city built on a hill cannot be hid. No one after lighting a lamp puts it under the bushel basket, but on the lampstand, and it gives light to all in the house. In the same way, let your light shine before others, so that they may see your good works and give glory to your Father in heaven."
Matthew 5:14–16

Read *Matthew 5:1–16* as well as *Psalm 19:1–6, Psalm 148,* and *Matthew 6:28–29.* What other things give glory to God?

_____

_____

Creativity

As humans we have the capabilities to build buildings, compose symphonies, and invent new technologies. But humans are not the only creatures with creative abilities— bees build hives, beavers build dams, and spiders weave webs. Families of whales use intricate songs to communicate with each other. However, intelligence and freedom brings human creativity to a much higher level.

The difference between how we create and how God created is even greater. God created the universe and everything in it from nothing. In other words, God did not make something out of something else. God created the universe freely and directly from nothing.

God did not create the universe as a finished product, however. The Church teaches that the universe was created "in a state of journeying." And we, as humans, have been invited to cooperate in that journey. This is where our creativity comes in.

While God is revealed in creation, he is distinct from creation; the universe is the universe, and God is God. Within creation, humans hold a special role. While we are not God, we share intimately in the life of God.

God lives in us, and we live in God. And more important, God loves us and desires our love in return.

God's life in us, freely given, is called **grace.** Through grace God communicates his presence and love. Grace helps us respond to God's call and be more like God, bringing the holiness of God together with the goodness of creation.

What has been your understanding of grace? Discuss your thoughts with your Faith Partner.

OUR CHRISTIAN JOURNEY

Evolution In his book *On the Origin of Species by Means of Natural Selection* Charles Darwin outlined the theory of evolution, proposing that all plants and animals are descended from earlier forms of plant and animal life. This theory caused a great deal of controversy in both religious and scientific communities. Now evolution is generally accepted by both of these communities. Although some religious groups continue to condemn this theory on the grounds that it disagrees with a literal interpretation of the Book of Genesis, most Jews and Christians accept the idea that God creates through the evolutionary process. In 1950 Pope Pius XII published the encyclical *Of the Human Race,* acknowledging the possibility of Darwin's theory.

For further information: Choose a scientific discovery, like evolution or an early medical practice, and research its effect on religious thought.

1850   1975

1859 ———
PUBLICATION OF *ON THE ORIGIN OF SPECIES*

1950 ———
PUBLICATION OF *OF THE HUMAN RACE*

1953 ———
MOUNT EVEREST CLIMBED FOR THE FIRST TIME

1961 ———
PEACE CORPS ESTABLISHED

The Glory of God

A story about Moses gives a hint about the awesome glory of God. In *Exodus 33:18–23* Moses asks for permission to view God's glory. According to the story, this request could be granted only partially; God knew that Moses would not survive the full revelation of God's beauty and power. When God passed by him, God shielded the face of Moses so the prophet would not be overcome.

God created the universe to show and communicate his glory, which his creatures would experience in truth, goodness, and beauty. To be fully human means being loving and loved, being joyful, concerned, and thankful, being one who serves others and one who receives. When we experience the many aspects of our lives, we see the vast goodness and glory of God, knowing that God has promised an even greater experience of his glory in heaven. Glory is the "why" of creation.

Catholics Believe

Every creature possesses its own goodness. Because of the goodness of all God's creation, people must respect all creatures, as well as the environment. See Catechism, #339.

What does this statement tell us about how people should interact with creation?

_____

_____

_____

Our Responsibility

God continues to energize all existence through his grace. His continued relationship with creation is called **providence,** which implies the Creator's ongoing care and protection. Understanding God's providence is not a simple matter, however, for human freedom and responsibility are also part of the equation.

To help clarify this concept, think of a play. We are not puppets in a play written and produced by God. Nor are we pawns in his chess game. We are free co-workers with God in bringing creation to its fulfillment.

Our human responsibility to care for creation is one of **stewardship.** A steward is someone who manages someone else's property or affairs, such as in Genesis when God leaves the first man in Eden to till the garden. (See *Genesis 2:15.*) The concept of stewardship acknowledges that we are not the owners of creation; God is. It also accepts the fact that, in our present mode of existence, we are part of the physical universe for a limited time and have a responsibility to preserve it for future generations.

The best way we can understand our responsibility as stewards of God's creation is to consider the **interdependence** of all of creation, first of all, in terms of how each species relies on other species.

God created great diversity in nature, with each creature having its own purpose and goodness. Modern science points out the immense importance of *biodiversity,* the variety of species within the ecosystems.

IN THE NEWS: THE ENVIRONMENT Over the course of the past few decades, news coverage of environmental issues has increased dramatically. To some extent this is due to the public's growing concern with environmental stewardship.

What environmental issues have you become aware of through the media? Indicate which of these issues are most important to you personally.

_____

_____

_____

There is goodness in all of creation, even in creatures we might usually think of as pests, such as mosquitoes. Wipe out the mosquito, and you've just eliminated the food source for many species of birds, fish, bats, and even a few reptiles. As good stewards we have a responsibility to help maintain the balance and diversity of nature.

Interdependence also describes the relationship of people relying upon and being responsible for each other. Just as diversity is important among various species, it is also important among humans. The cultural diversity of our own society strengthens us and adds to our level of creativity. A huge part of our responsibility as stewards of God's creation is to recognize the goodness of all people, regardless of race, gender, or religious belief. In this way we become aware of the special way in which God is revealed through humans, those members of creation fashioned in God's own image and likeness.

Stewards of Creation

Mother Teresa of Calcutta had a simple solution to the demand for stewardship: "Live simply, so that others can simply live." This is a tough message to consider, living as we do in a society where consumerism is seen as a good thing. But do we *really* need all the stuff we are able to purchase? How many pairs of sneakers does one person need when there are people who have no shoes to wear?

Another way to become stewards for creation is by studying and analyzing environmental issues, both local and worldwide. Knowledge is power. Knowing about problems can show us where and how to live more simply. If we know about rain-forest destruction, we can target and avoid products that, by their existence, harm the rain-forest ecosystem by depleting certain resources.

But living more simply and becoming aware of environmental issues is not enough. We also need to take action. You don't have to be an adult before you can begin to do something positive for the environment. In fact, young adults and children have taught many adults about recycling, conserving energy, using less, and eliminating waste.

Stewardship represents our duty to care for the earth. Respecting and caring for the earth and its diversity is an important way we glorify God.

Reflect on ways you can be a steward of God's creation. Share your thoughts with your Faith Partner.

FAITH PARTNERSHIP

WRAP UP

- God created the universe freely and directly, from nothing.
- The universe was created in a "state of journeying."
- God, in his providence, continues to care for all creation.
- Stewardship is our responsibility to care for creation.
- Diversity and interdependence are two values that flow from creation.

What questions do you have about the information presented in this chapter?

_____

_____

_____

Around the Group

Discuss the following question as a group.

What specific action can you do as a group to be stewards of creation?

After everyone has had a chance to share his or her responses, come up with a group answer upon which everyone can agree.

_____

_____

_____

_____

What personal observations do you have about the group discussion and answer?

_____

_____

_____

_____

Briefly. . .

Based on what you have learned about stewardship and the glory of God, how would you change your headlines from the *What Do You Think?* activity on page 25? If you do not need to change a headline, explain why.

_____

_____

_____

Giving Thanks

Expressions of Faith—

When we observe the wonders of creation, we see that there is much for which we are thankful. The skill of Giving Thanks requires us to recognize the loving actions we see happening around us and to show gratitude for them. In addition, giving thanks is one way that we can remind ourselves of the goodness of life, especially at times when it seems that bad news surrounds us.

Scripture

Rejoice always, pray without ceasing, give thanks in all circumstances; for this is the will of God in Christ Jesus for you.
1 Thessalonians 5:16—18

3rd Sunday of Advent, Cycle B

Think About It—

How could the young people in the following examples have done a better job of giving thanks?

○ Bobbie's mom drives Rita home from the school field trip. Rita gets out of the car and heads for her house. Rita's mom says, "Did you thank Mrs. Brown?" Rita continues into the house, with her back to the Browns' car and says, "Thanks," just before the door closes behind her.

_____

_____

_____

○ Ray is on the couch watching TV when his dad comes home from the hospital. His dad announces that Grandma is recovering from surgery and that she does not have cancer. Ray continues watching the TV program and simply says, "Neat."

_____

_____

_____

Skill Steps-

One way to remember the skill of Giving Thanks is to remember the letter *S. Stop. Smile. Say something. Store it.* Stopping is a respectful way of honoring the situation. Smiling is a concrete way of displaying appreciation. Saying something enables us to make personal contact with the person we are thanking. (You don't always have to express your thanks with words; you can also use a gesture or a small gift.) Storing the memory of the kindness is helpful during the times you forget how kind someone can be, the good things in life, or the blessings of God.

Check It Out-

Place a check mark next to the sentences that apply to you.

○ I usually stop what I'm doing when I express thanks.

○ I look someone in the eye and smile when I give thanks.

○ My family would give me a good grade for the frequency and manner in which I give thanks.

○ My friends would give me a good grade for the frequency and manner in which I give thanks.

○ I make it a point to deliberately express my gratitude with words or a gesture when I give thanks.

○ I find myself easily remembering events, moments, or relationships for which I give thanks.

Based on your responses, what are your strong points, and what areas do you need to work on?

_____

_____

Closing Prayer-

Thank you, Lord, for the many blessings you give us. Thank you for life, and thank you for revealing your love to us. Help us grow as stewards of creation.

CHAPTER
4

A Mystery
of Faith

God our Father,
we thank you
for revealing
yourself to us
in so many
ways, especially
through your
Son, Jesus,
and your
Holy Spirit.
Help us know
you better.

Below is a list of roles that might describe your relationship to other people. Circle three of these terms that apply to you. Then explain how people who know you in one role might describe you differently from someone who knows you in a different role.

classmate	sister or brother	grandchild
leader	group member	student
teammate	son or daughter	baby-sitter
assistant	hobbyist	expert
friend	teacher	coach

_____

_____

_____

_____

Beyond
Understanding

Our images of God are limited. Our minds are just not capable of imagining the greatness of God's love and power, just as our language doesn't contain enough words to adequately describe him.

Think about personal pronouns, such as he, she, or me. What personal pronoun can we use to describe God? We believe that the reality of God is beyond gender, and yet our language tends to both help and limit us by referring to God with personal pronouns. But any of these pronouns are insufficient as a description for God.

Saint Augustine summed up the inadequacy of our language eloquently in one of his sermons, where he said, "If you understood him, it would not be God."

The Unexplained

Can you think of things in the world around you that seem unexplainable? Perhaps you have studied natural phenomena, such as tornadoes or DNA, or the architecture of ancient civilizations, such as the Great Wall of China. And even if you have gained some understanding about these wonders, there are some aspects that remain unexplained.

The same is true of our relationship with and knowledge of God. A **mystery** is a truth about faith that we cannot fully understand but believe because God revealed it.

Opening the Word

Jesus said to them, "Very truly, I tell you, the Son can do nothing on his own, . . . for whatever the Father does, the Son does likewise. The Father loves the Son and shows him all that he himself is doing; and he will show him greater works than these, so that you will be astonished." John 5:19–20

Read *John 5:19–30* as well as *Matthew 11:25–27* and *Mark 12:1–12.* In what ways is the work of the Father and the Son similar? In what ways is their work different?

_____

_____

_____

"If you understood him, it would not be God."

— Saint Augustine

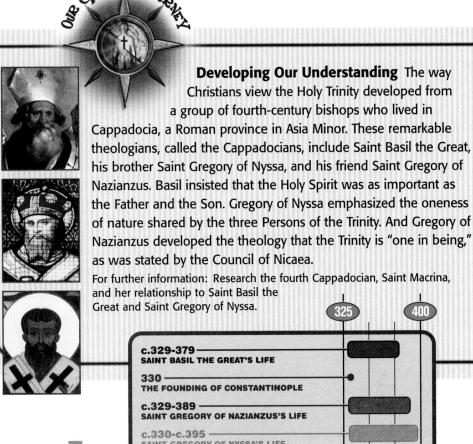

Developing Our Understanding The way Christians view the Holy Trinity developed from a group of fourth-century bishops who lived in Cappadocia, a Roman province in Asia Minor. These remarkable theologians, called the Cappadocians, include Saint Basil the Great, his brother Saint Gregory of Nyssa, and his friend Saint Gregory of Nazianzus. Basil insisted that the Holy Spirit was as important as the Father and the Son. Gregory of Nyssa emphasized the oneness of nature shared by the three Persons of the Trinity. And Gregory of Nazianzus developed the theology that the Trinity is "one in being," as was stated by the Council of Nicaea.

For further information: Research the fourth Cappadocian, Saint Macrina, and her relationship to Saint Basil the Great and Saint Gregory of Nyssa.

325   400

c.329-379 —
SAINT BASIL THE GREAT'S LIFE

330 —
THE FOUNDING OF CONSTANTINOPLE

c.329-389 —
SAINT GREGORY OF NAZIANZUS'S LIFE

c.330-c.395 —
SAINT GREGORY OF NYSSA'S LIFE

Church
Teaching About
the Trinity

The **Holy Trinity,** our belief in one God in three divine Persons, is the central mystery of the Catholic faith. It is a belief that distinguishes us from many of the other religions of the world. But we don't completely understand the Trinity. How can God be one and at the same time three—Father, Son, and Holy Spirit?

One of the problems in arriving at an understanding of the Trinity comes from the use of the word *Persons*. This term was introduced somewhat gradually into Christianity and is not used at all within the New Testament. Our understanding of the word *person* makes it

more difficult to understand this mystery. Perhaps the best way of visualizing the three Persons of the Trinity is to recognize that there have been three distinct ways God has gradually revealed himself in salvation history. This is true despite the fact that God has one will and is "one in being."

The first revelation of God is as Creator. In Christian understanding this is God the Father. Then God revealed himself in Jesus, the Son of God and second Person of the Holy Trinity, who is Redeemer. Jesus then promised the Holy Spirit, the third Person of the Holy Trinity, who is the Spirit of Truth and our Advocate.

Catholics Believe

Although we usually credit the work of creation to the Father, it is equally true that the Father, the Son, and the Holy Spirit participate together in the process of creation. See Catechism, #316.

What does this statement tell us about the oneness of the Holy Trinity?

_____

_____

_____

_____

_____

Each person of the Holy Trinity is God, whole and entire. In knowing Jesus, we know the Father. (See *John 14:7.*) In seeing Jesus, we see the Father. (See *John 14:9.*) In experiencing the love of the Holy Spirit, we experience the love of the Father and the Son. We should not think of God as being *divided* among the Trinity. Rather, the *revelation* of God is *multiplied.* We proclaim in the Nicene Creed that Jesus proceeds from the Father, and yet we believe that Jesus and the Holy Spirit were one with the Father in the act of creation. Likewise, we proclaim that the Holy Spirit proceeds from the Father and the Son. Jesus is the way, the truth, and the life through which the Father can be known. The Holy Spirit at work in the Church reveals Christ today.

In reality the mystery of God is beyond the capacity of our minds. Not only is the doctrine of the Holy Trinity a sacred mystery, but God himself—Father, Son, and Holy Spirit—is mystery. In fact, mystery is an appropriate way to think of God. Native Americans of the Sioux Nation have a name for God that captures this truth. They call the creator *Wakan Tanka,* or "Great Mystery."

FaiTH PaRTNeRSHip

Together with your Faith Partner, write a prayer that highlights God as three Persons.

An Unknown God

The second half of the Acts of the Apostles tells about the missionary journeys of Saint Paul. One of these journeys took Paul to the Greek city of Athens, where his preaching met with great success. When Paul made his way to the public square of Athens, he was met by philosophers, who gathered there for daily debates.

Paul told these philosophers that he noticed how religious they were, with so many shrines to different gods throughout the city.

He told them that he had seen an altar inscribed "To an unknown god." (See *Acts 17:23.*) Then Paul told the Athenians who this unknown god was—the Lord of heaven and earth.

Christianity is something more than just a philosophy about God. It is more than a system of beliefs about the divine. Instead, it is a way of directly experiencing God in word, sacrament, and community.

The mystery of the Trinity means that the God who created us, who redeemed us, who sustains us, and who offers us eternal life is close to us and continues to be present in our history. God's revelation and work in the world is constant—yesterday, today, and tomorrow.

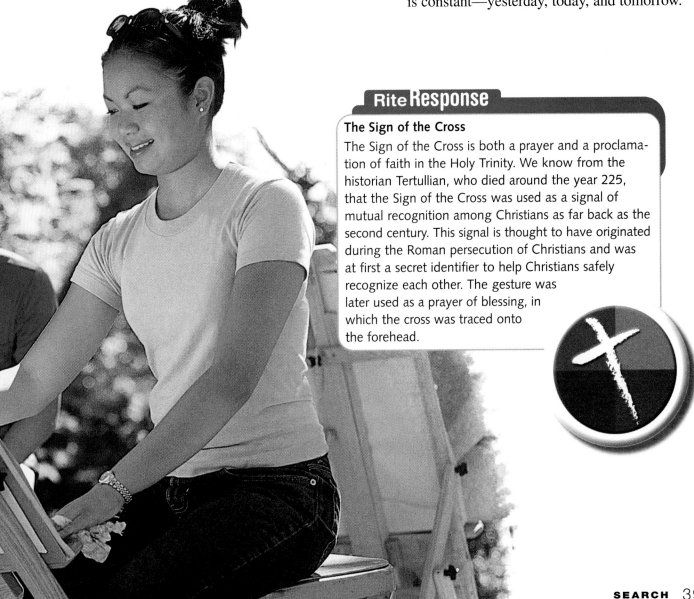

Rite Response

The Sign of the Cross

The Sign of the Cross is both a prayer and a proclamation of faith in the Holy Trinity. We know from the historian Tertullian, who died around the year 225, that the Sign of the Cross was used as a signal of mutual recognition among Christians as far back as the second century. This signal is thought to have originated during the Roman persecution of Christians and was at first a secret identifier to help Christians safely recognize each other. The gesture was later used as a prayer of blessing, in which the cross was traced onto the forehead.

A Reflection of Love

The Trinity is three Persons in one God, one in being with each other. The union of the Holy Trinity is described as "the communion of three Persons."

A medieval theologian, Richard of Saint Victor, wrote that the beginning point in understanding the Trinity is to understand human nature. He reflected on the unselfish love of human friendship as a reflection of the love found within the communion of the Holy Trinity. He attempted to understand the Trinity as one infinite love in the form of three Persons, all of whom love without ceasing.

Because the love of neighbor is inseparable from the love of God, the Church teaches that there is a "certain resemblance" between the communion of the Holy Trinity and human community. There are many examples of this resemblance in our lives. A marriage ceremony is a union of shared love. This union is celebrated within the Church as well as within our families and with other community members. This celebration not only brings God and his grace into the relationship between the man and woman being joined in marriage, but also to the other people present. When we come together in love, we experience God more profoundly because God is love.

Reflect on events in your life when you have experienced a unity that mirrors the communion of the Trinity. Share your thoughts with your Faith Partner.

FaiTH ParTNeRSHiP

WRAP UP

- **A mystery is a truth of our faith that we cannot fully understand but which we believe because God has revealed it.**
- **The Holy Trinity is the central mystery of Christianity.**
- **Each Person of the Trinity is God, whole and entire.**
- **The primary way Christians come to know the Father is through knowing Jesus.**
- **Through the Holy Spirit we can come to know God through word, sacrament, and community.**

What questions do you have about the information presented in this chapter?

_____

_____

_____

Around the Group

Discuss the following question as a group.

A symbol that has been commonly used to explain the Holy Trinity is the shamrock. What other symbol or analogy can you think of that expresses the Trinity?

After everyone has had a chance to share his or her responses, come up with a group symbol or analogy upon which everyone can agree.

_____
_____
_____
_____

What personal observations do you have about the group discussion and symbol or analogy?

_____
_____
_____
_____
_____

Briefly...

At the beginning of this chapter, you were asked to describe your relationship to others. Based on what you have learned, what words would you use to describe your relationship to the Trinity? Explain your answers.

_____
_____
_____

Giving Thanks

Expressions of Faith–

The mystery of the Trinity can continue to bring you many blessings. In the first two chapters, you were introduced to the skill of Recognizing God's Presence. The skill of Giving Thanks involves having the eyes and ears to notice the blessings of God all around you.

Skill Steps–

Giving thanks is a way of responding to God once we have experienced the revelation of God's love. Remember that there are four steps in Giving Thanks. Here are some key points to remember:

- Giving thanks is a response to recognizing God's presence in truth, beauty, and love.
- Giving thanks helps you recognize goodness in a world that can be cruel.
- Giving thanks makes others feel appreciated.

Stop
Smile
Say something
STORE IT

Skill Builder–

Read through the situations presented below, and try to come up with a creative way that you could express thanks.

- You have fallen behind in a class due to illness and have been given several opportunities to catch up by meeting with the teacher after school.

  _____

- A teammate's parents always bring a cooler full of drinks for you to enjoy after the soccer game.

  _____

- A friend has two free movie passes and invites you to come along.

  _____

Share your responses and thoughts with your Faith Partner.

Faith Partnership

Putting It into Practice-

Take a moment to think about everything that has happened to you in the past week. Think back over your schedule on a day-by-day basis, including the weekend. As you do this, remember things that have happened to you for which you are thankful. Make a list with at least seven events, one for each day of the week.

_____

_____

_____

_____

_____

_____

_____

_____

_____

After you have completed the list, choose one of the events for which you would like to give thanks, either to God or to another person involved, and decide upon a way to express your gratitude.

   Giving thanks can also help you in difficult times. The next time you feel sad, frustrated, or overwhelmed, focus on the good in your life and give thanks. The memories that will come to you can balance out the tough times in your life and give you hope.

Where are you in the skill of Giving Thanks? Give yourself a grade (*A* through *F*) _____. **Write one way you can improve your grade next week.**

_____

_____

Closing Prayer-

*We give you **thanks**, Lord in the name of the Father, who created us, and of the Son, who redeemed us, and of the Holy Spirit, who sanctifies us.*

CHAPTER 5

The God of Abraham

God of

Abraham,

we thank you

for keeping

your promises.

Help us better

understand

your steadfast

love, and guide

us in our search

for the wisdom

of the ages.

In each of the five spaces below, write the name of a value that is important to you. Try to use a single word, such as *honesty*, to identify each of these values.

_____   _____

_____   _____

_____

Review the values you have listed. Circle the ones that you feel were primarily taught to you by your parents or other family members. Next to any of the values not circled, write the name of the person or group from whom you learned it.

The Inheritance of Faith

Jews, Christians, and Muslims trace their ancestry back to Abraham. Yet in a very real way, everyone who acknowledges the one God is in some way a son or daughter of Abraham, for we have all inherited his faith.

According to the best scholarly estimates, the story of Abraham has been passed along from one generation to the

next for nearly forty centuries. On the day Abraham was born, human civilization had not yet developed an alphabet, nor had the first tools been fashioned of iron.

The Great Pyramids of Egypt, built for religious reasons, were already 400 years old at the time of Abraham. But Abraham is remembered for a form of religious observance known as *monotheism,* the worship of one God. Through Abraham we know that God, who is one, wished to have a relationship with people. This belief changed the course of civilization.

Covenant and Relationship

When a man and a woman have romantic feelings for each other, they sometimes decide to "see" only each other. This mutual decision is a promise by both people not to "see" others as long as they're going together, but it is understood that the decision can be changed by either individual for any reason at any point in the relationship.

A marriage vow is a more permanent promise. At a marriage ceremony each person vows to love the other regardless of conditions ("in good times and in bad") for as long as both persons live. A sacred, binding promise between two parties is called a **covenant.**

In modern society, agreements are written on paper and signed by the parties involved. Such agreements are called *contracts*. In early Hebrew society, agreements were formalized by speaking the words of the promises and sometimes by a type of ritual, such as an animal sacrifice.

"Hear, O Israel: The LORD is our God, the LORD alone."

Deuteronomy 6:4

Opening the Word

Sacred Heart of Jesus, Cycle A

For you are a people holy to the LORD your God; the LORD your God has chosen you out of all the peoples on earth to be his people, his treasured possession. Deuteronomy 7:6

Read *Deuteronomy 7* as well as *Genesis 17:1–14, Exodus 24:3–8*, and *Psalm 89:20–37.* What similar aspects of the covenant are expressed in all of these passages?

_____

_____

_____

There are many covenants mentioned in the Old Testament. Most of these are between people, usually involving peace treaties or agreements regarding borders. The most important, life-changing covenant mentioned in the Old Testament is the covenant God established with his people.

The story of Abraham, found in the Book of Genesis, begins with his call by God. (See *Genesis 12:1–9.*) Abraham's story is one of covenant and faith. Abraham's faith in God was so strong that he was willing to sacrifice his only son, Isaac, because he believed that was what God wanted. God stopped him from making that sacrifice, however, and was so impressed with Abraham's faith that he made a covenant with Abraham. God promised that the descendants of Abraham would become "as numerous as the stars of heaven and as the sand that is on the seashore" *(Genesis 22:17–18).*

This covenant was renewed and expanded upon with Moses during the Exodus, the Israelites' forty-year journey from slavery to the promised land. At this time the Hebrew people promised to uphold the Law that God revealed to Moses on Mount Sinai.

The promise that God made as part of the covenant with Moses was a simple one: I will be your God; you will be my people. (See *Leviticus 26:12.*) It is because of this covenant that the Jewish people are called the chosen people of God. Their special relationship with YHWH, a covenant relationship, continues to this day and will never be withdrawn.

With your Faith Partner, discuss the covenant with God and its meaning for all of us.

FaiTH PaRTNeRSHiP

Living by the Law of Love

Maximilian Mary Kolbe was born January 8, 1894, in Russian-occupied Poland. He grew up poor in a devout family of cottage weavers. When he was fourteen years old, he joined the Franciscan Order. At eighteen he was sent to Rome, where he studied theology and philosophy. There, along with six other students, he formed an organization devoted to the Virgin Mary and dedicated to spreading the Catholic faith.

Kolbe's organization grew to the point where it was publishing nine journals read by a great number of people. When World War II broke out, he sent most of his friars away, but he remained in Poland, sheltering Jews. Kolbe was soon arrested and was interned in Auschwitz, a German concentration camp. When one man escaped, ten men were chosen to starve to death. Kolbe volunteered to take the place of a young father. In 1981 Pope John Paul II canonized Maximilian Kolbe as a martyr who faithfully lived the law of love to the end.

For further information: Research the life of another martyr of faith. How did his or her life reflect the law of love?

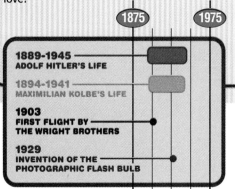

1875   1975

1889–1945
ADOLF HITLER'S LIFE

1894–1941
MAXIMILIAN KOLBE'S LIFE

1903
FIRST FLIGHT BY THE WRIGHT BROTHERS

1929
INVENTION OF THE PHOTOGRAPHIC FLASH BULB

The Will of God

To understand the renewal of the covenant at Sinai, it is important to note that this renewal included obligations placed on the people. These obligations are called *the Law,* which is more properly called the Torah.

In addition to civil matters, the Torah also contains a code of holiness, which includes various moral laws. It deals as well with festivals, sacrifices, dietary practices, the conduct of priests, and the prohibition of idol worship.

What is unique about the Torah, when compared to the laws of other cultures of the same era, is the concept of the Law as being from God. Other legal codes are of human origin. The concept of the Law as a sacred covenant with God is also unique to the Torah. And the motivation to observe the Law is different because it begins with religious obligation rather than a need to live peaceably within a society's rules.

One of the earliest controversies facing the Christian Church was whether the followers of Jesus were obliged to observe the Torah. This was especially a concern for the many Gentiles (non-Jews) who converted to the Christian faith. The Acts of the Apostles reports that, after significant debate, it was decided that three Jewish practices from the Torah would be imposed upon followers of Jesus: that they abstain from meat sacrificed to idols, that they not consume blood, and that they not engage in illicit sexual union. (See *Acts 15:29*.)

Christianity has always taught the core of the Torah. This core for living a moral life is known as the **Decalogue,** or Ten Commandments. The first three of these commandments deal with religious life: not worshiping idols, not taking the name of God in vain, and keeping the Lord's Day holy. Next comes a commandment to honor one's parents. Following that are prohibitions against killing, committing adultery, stealing, bearing false witness, desiring someone else's things, and desiring someone else's husband or wife.

Why We Follow

We do not view the Decalogue as the only norm for all moral decisions. It barely touches upon individual moral obligations, such as the importance of being merciful or generous. The focus of the Decalogue, rather, is the welfare of the whole community, and it prohibits those actions that injure the community. As such, it is more than an ethical document. Instead, it is a religious testimony to the covenant bond between God and Israel.

To the Jews the covenant is the constant motivation for keeping the Law. God is revealed through the Torah, which means that the covenant is more than just a contract. The bond of the covenant is greater; it is a bond establishing a kinship between two parties—God and his people. The affection established with YHWH through the covenant is the same sort of affection felt between family members.

God promised David that a descendant of David would establish David's kingdom forever. Christians believe that Jesus is this descendant of David and that he established God's kingdom on earth forever.

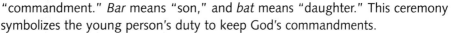

Our Global Community

A Jewish Ceremony

When Jewish boys are thirteen years old, they participate in a ceremony called a *bar mitzvah.* In the non-Orthodox Jewish communities, girls of twelve or thirteen participate in *bat mitzvah.* In Hebrew the word *mitzvah* means "commandment." *Bar* means "son," and *bat* means "daughter." This ceremony symbolizes the young person's duty to keep God's commandments.

During a bar or bat mitzvah, the young person leads all or part of the Jewish Sabbath services, called *Shabbat.* The key part of the ceremony is when the young person reads from the Torah. He or she might also lead other parts of the service, including some of the traditional chants.

Taking on the responsibility of faith practice is also a part of the Catholic faith tradition which is celebrated in the Sacraments of Christian Initiation.

Faithfulness

The Jewish experience of God is one of mercy and fidelity. YHWH is a God who never abandons his people. Religion, to a Jew, is as much about faithfulness as it is about faith. It is a matter of maintaining an ancient tradition of faithfulness to God by observing the commandments, maintaining hope while celebrating the Sabbath and holy days, and remembering the practices of the covenant. All of this together is what is meant by their Law, the Torah.

Catholic faith is rooted in the Jewish experience of God. The beliefs are different, as are our practices, but the call to a life of holiness is one and the same. There is a great deal we can learn about the life of faith from the Jewish people, especially regarding the virtue of faithfulness.

The Law is not what we *must* do in order for God to love us, but rather it is a summary of how we live in relationship with God and with others as a natural extension of our faithfulness. For instance, if your friend receives a desirable present, such as a mountain bike, you don't want to envy your friend's possession of it or desire it for yourself. If you love and respect your friend, you will be happy for him or her and you won't need to remind yourself not to want the bike. In the same way, we learn that having a relationship with God is first of all a matter of observing various laws *and* a matter of being faithful to a covenant with God.

Reflect on how we can be faithful to our covenant with God. Share your thoughts with your Faith Partner.

FaiTH PaRTNeRSHiP

WRAP UP

- Abraham is remembered for a form of religious observance known as monotheism, the worship of one God.

- The sacred, binding promise joining God and people in relationship is known as a covenant.

- God's covenant with the Jewish people is, I will be your God; you will be my people.

- We are all called to a life of holiness by God who will never abandon us.

What questions do you have about the information presented in this chapter?

_____

_____

_____

THE TEN COMMANDMENTS

1. I am the Lord your God. You shall not have stra...

2. You shall not take the nam...

3. Remember to keep holy th...

4. Honor your father and your mother.

5. You shall not...

6. You shall no...

7. You shall n...

You shall not bear false witness against your neighbor.

9. You shall not covet your neighbor's wife.

10. You shall not covet your neighbor's goods.

Around the Group

Discuss the following question as a group.

If you could add one commandment to the Ten Commandments, what would it be?

After everyone has had a chance to share his or her responses, come up with a group answer upon which everyone can agree.

_____

_____

_____

_____

What personal observations do you have about the group discussion and answer?

_____

_____

_____

_____

Briefly...

At the beginning of this chapter, you were asked to identify values. Based upon what you have learned about the God of Abraham, how will the covenant influence your own values?

_____

_____

_____

Letting Go

Expressions of Faith

Part of being faithful is developing the confidence that faith can carry us through hardships of every sort. We come to realize that our faith sometimes calls us to accept what life brings us and to let go of it. The skill of Letting Go involves managing our emotions in a certain way and putting our difficulties in God's hands.

Scripture

Now faith is the assurance of things hoped for, the conviction of things not seen. Indeed, by faith our ancestors received approval.

Hebrews 11:1–2   19th Sunday of Ordinary Time, Cycle C

Think About It

Join with a partner to list the effects of each person's reluctance toward letting go in the different situations given below.

⊙ Erica was cut from the basketball team. All of her best friends made the team. She is sure that politics were involved in her being cut. She tells other classmates that two girls made the team only because their parents are good friends with the coach.

_____

_____

_____

⊙ Six months ago Tim moved to another state. He has not tried to make new friends. Instead he e-mails his old friends. He says he is bored and unhappy. He is mad at his parents for moving.

_____

_____

_____

_____

_____

_____

Skill Steps-

Although difficult, the skill of Letting Go is one of the most important Skills for Christian living. Like the other skills dealing with emotions, Letting Go involves managing emotions through using *Name it; Tame it; Claim it.*

Name it. Identify exactly what emotion you are feeling (mad, sad, embarrassed, happy).

Tame it. Manage your emotions by releasing them to God and saying good-bye to the feelings you are holding on to. At the same time, even though you may not understand why something happened or why you feel the way you do, you need to trust and say hello to what God may be bringing forward to you. However, don't rush the good-bye or force a new hello. Take time to sit with your emotions.

Claim it. Make this a productive experience for yourself by seeing what you can learn from it or how it can help you better understand the pain of others.

Check It Out-

Place a check mark next to the sentences that apply to you.

○ I tend not to dwell on things that go wrong.

○ I am able to forgive those who have harmed me.

○ There are people with whom I can talk about emotional issues.

○ I am usually able to move on emotionally once I've dealt with a situation.

○ My faith is an asset to me in the process of letting go.

Based on your responses, what do you want to remember about letting go?

_____

_____

_____

Closing Prayer-

God of Abraham, thank you for being faithful to your promises. Help us develop the skill of Letting Go, and remind us of your presence when we are troubled.

God our Father,
we thank you
for loving us
so much that
you sent us
your Son.
Help us follow
his teachings
all the days
of our lives.

God's Only Son

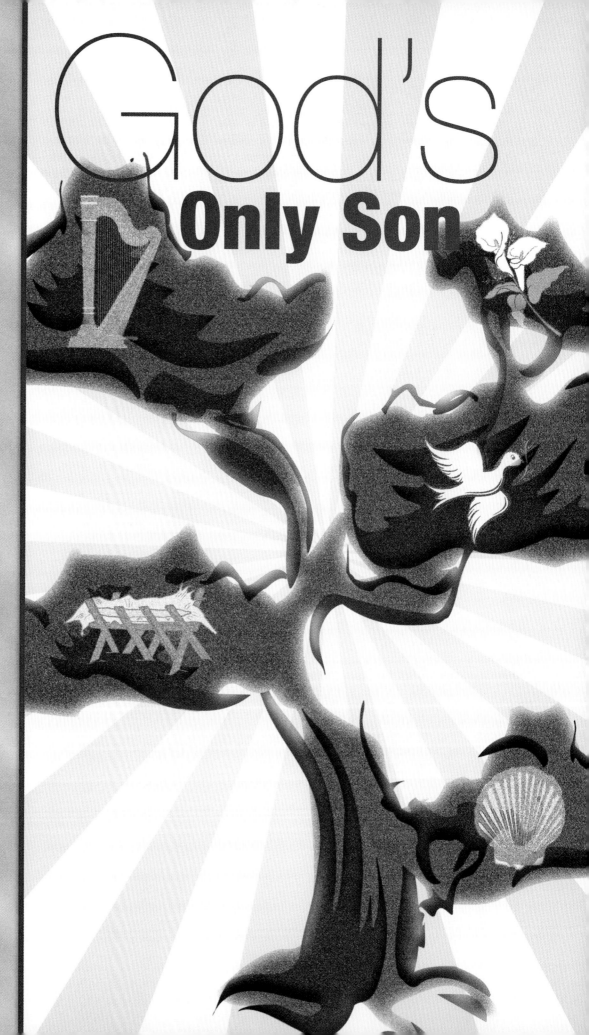

What Do You Think?

Jesus has been portrayed in a greater variety of ways than any other figure in history. Which one of the portraits below most closely matches your own image of Jesus? Circle that picture, and then write the reasons for your selection.

Longing for the Messiah

Think of a time when someone special was coming to visit. Maybe a favorite uncle was visiting from another state. Or perhaps your best friend who moved away was returning for the holidays. What were your emotions when you learned about the visit? What about on the day before the visit? Anticipation can be very exciting and even mysterious as you wonder about what the visitor will look like now or how much fun you'll have.

Now imagine you live in the time before Jesus. All your life you have heard about the messiah. All your life you and many of the people in your community have longed to meet the messiah. Can you imagine the feelings you would have? You would hope for and anticipate the great event.

Saying "Yes" to **God**

When the Son of God became man, God became visible to humanity. This does not mean that God ceased to be a mystery, but rather that God revealed himself in new ways as he became one of us. The **incarnation** is the mystery of the Son of God becoming human.

The Gospel according to Luke tells us that in the days of Herod, the king of Judea, the angel Gabriel, a messenger from God, was sent to the town of Nazareth in Galilee. There Gabriel announced to a young woman named Mary that she had "found favor with God." During this event, called the **annunciation,** the angel told Mary that God had chosen her to conceive and bear a son who would be named Jesus.

All of salvation history since creation had led up to this moment. The Son of God would become a human on earth. At first Mary was troubled. Having free will, Mary could have said "no," but she didn't. Her answer, or **fiat,** was to say "yes" to God. She responded, "Here am I, the servant of the Lord; let it be with me according to your word" *(Luke 1:38).*

In *Luke 1:46–55* we read Mary's song of praise to God, called the **Magnificat,** or Canticle of Mary. In a very real way, Mary's "yes" was the beginning of her cooperation with the salvation brought by Jesus.

Media Message

THE MAGNIFICAT Taken from the Latin word meaning "to magnify," *Magnificat* is the title given to Mary's canticle of praise. It is a song of praise and a beautiful prayer for anyone struggling to respond to God's call. The Magnificat has been put to music many times, in various forms from folk music to Gregorian chant. Many classical composers have written music to accompany the Magnificat, including Telemann, Bach, Schubert, and Vivaldi. The Magnificat has even been performed as a ballet.

What type of artistic representation would you use to portray the Magnificat? Sketch out below an image, or brainstorm ideas for another form of art, such as music or dance.

The Second Person of the Trinity

Jesus is like us in all things but sin. Because sin is separation from God, Jesus, though fully human, could not in any way be separated from God. In fact, while he was fully human by nature of his birth, he was also fully divine, one in being with God the Father. In choosing to take on a human nature, Jesus chose to share in our mortality, to accept death even though he did not have original sin and did not sin. As Savior, Jesus freely chose to save us from the power of sin, which separates us from God.

Jesus reconciled God and humans in two ways. First, through the incarnation, humanity and divinity became one in Jesus. Second, through his suffering, death, and resurrection, Jesus opened for us the way to a new life in God, now and forever.

What difference does it make to you that Jesus was fully human and fully divine? Share your thoughts with your Faith Partner.

Our Christian Journey

375		475

c.390–c.461
SAINT PATRICK'S LIFE

425
UNIVERSITY OF CONSTANTINOPLE FOUNDED

431
COUNCIL OF EPHESUS

c.450
BOWS AND ARROWS FIRST USED FOR HUNTING IN NORTH AMERICA

Settling Controversy An ecumenical council is a gathering of the bishops of the entire Church. The Council of Ephesus met in A.D. 431. The members of this council dealt with several controversies within the Church. One of these issues was whether Mary could truly be called the Mother of God. It was decided that this title was indeed appropriate because "It was not an ordinary man who was first born of the holy virgin, and upon whom afterwards the Word descended, but [God] himself, united to humanity from the womb, is said to have undergone fleshly birth."

For further information: Research to find out the other issues dealt with during the Council of Ephesus.

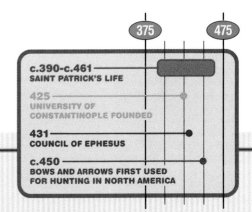

More Than Just a Savior

Christ's birth, death, and resurrection are central events in our salvation history. Jesus not only taught us about the nature of God; he *is* God. "I am the way, and the truth, and the life" *(John 14:6).*

The focus of Jesus' teaching is the reign of God. And he taught about the reign of God through the words of the parables and his healing actions.

Within the reign of God, things are not always the way humans think. The last are first, and the mighty are humbled. The poor in spirit are blessed, and the sorrowing are comforted. With these contradictions to ordinary thinking, Jesus shows us that in God's eyes the things that we might consider important are not necessarily so. We open ourselves to joy if we let go of our attachments to things that are only of this world. For example, imagine you could own every CD that you want. Now imagine that in order to do so, you cannot share the music with anyone. Only you could listen to that music, and no one else would have any idea of how it sounded. Now suppose that you have only one CD, but you can share the music. You can invite friends over to dance, or you can play your favorite song for your classmates during lunch. Owning many CDs is a material desire. Wanting to share the joy of the CD you have is a selfless act. The difference is the intention.

Catholics Believe

The Word became flesh so we could partake in the divine nature of God. See Catechism, #460.

How do you feel when you think about Jesus' role in our reconciliation with God?

_____

_____

_____

Just as Jesus is the sacrament, or sign, of God's love for us, we are, in turn, sacraments of Christ's presence for others. Through the teachings of Jesus, we come to understand the intimate connection between the love of God and the love of neighbor. It is about becoming fully alive in God, recognizing God within ourselves and others, and acting on that. By treating ourselves and others with respect and love, we acknowledge the dignity that has been given by God to each person.

The reign of God has not yet been fully revealed. The great mystery of our faith is that Christ came to live among us, Christ has died, Christ is risen, and Christ will come again. Even though the reign of God is already present, we pray "your kingdom come" in the knowledge that the fulfillment of the kingdom is yet to be.

As Christians and followers of Christ, we are not to passively await Christ's return at the end of time. Rather, we need to follow the inspiration of Mary's fiat. Just as Mary helped bring Christ to this world, we can help bring Jesus to those around us by representing Christ to them—living by his teachings and loving as he did.

Remember that Mary's fiat was not the only "yes" involved in the incarnation. In the Gospel according to Matthew, we are told how Joseph, upon discovering that Mary, to whom he was engaged, was pregnant, had decided to break off the engagement. An angel of the Lord appeared to him in a dream and told him not to fear, that Mary had conceived by the power of the Holy Spirit. Joseph married her, and Jesus was thus born into the family of King David; the prophecies of the messiah were fulfilled. All people who say "yes" to God as a sign of their faith are signs of the kingdom of God.

Opening the Word

Christmas Day Mass

And the Word became flesh and lived among us, and we have seen his glory, the glory as of a father's only son, full of grace and truth.
John 1:14

Read *John 1:10–18* as well as *Isaiah 9:6, Isaiah 11:1–9,* and *Luke 2:1–20.* Note the similarities between these texts regarding the birth of the Messiah. What are some of the emotions mentioned?

_____

_____

_____

Finding Our **Response**

Mary has been seen as the perfect example of responding to God's call. If we reexamine the story of the annunciation, we discover emotional elements in Mary's response. She showed fear when the angel appeared to her, and yet she did not allow her fear to take over. She also expressed confusion at being told that she would bear a son, and yet she was willing to listen to a further explanation of the subject.

One of the first steps for all of us, in responding to God's call, is to face our fears. We may fear a range of things, from being made fun of to failing. When we sense that God is calling us to perform a task, we need to respond by focusing on our abilities and the strategies we might use to complete the task. We should not focus on our weaknesses or the difficulties involved. Perhaps you are uncomfortable speaking in front of a group of people. But you worked on your presentation for weeks, and you knew it was more than just good enough; it was excellent. If, prior to your speech, you reflect on the fact that you are prepared and have done a good job, you might be less likely to fear appearing foolish in front of the class.

Like Mary, we should also be honest about our own confusion. It is not easy to know how God is calling us or what God is calling us to do. But if we share our confusion with God in prayer, over a period of time the picture will become clear. God will help us understand.

Reflect on the ways you can respond to God in your life. Share your thoughts with your Faith Partner.

FaiTH ParTNeRSHiP

WRAP UP

- **When the Son of God became man, God became visible to humanity.**
- **Mary is the Mother of God.**
- **By his death Christ redeemed us and restored our relationship with God.**
- **The focus of Jesus' teaching was the reign of God.**
- **The reign of God is the fulfillment of our humanity.**

What questions do you have about the information presented in this chapter?

_____

_____

_____

Around the Group

Discuss the following question as a group.

Why is it sometimes difficult to say "yes" to God?

After everyone has had a chance to share his or her responses, come up with a group answer upon which everyone can agree.

_____

_____

_____

_____

What personal observations do you have about the group discussion and answer?

_____

_____

_____

_____

Briefly. . .

At the beginning of this chapter, you were asked to select a portrait of Jesus that most closely matched your own image of him. How has your image of Jesus changed based on what you have learned about the incarnation?

_____

_____

_____

Letting Go

Expressions of Faith-

Jesus, in his human nature, had to overcome real fears. In the Gospel according to Mark, we are told about Jesus' prayer in the Garden of Gethsemane the night before his crucifixion. Jesus had told his disciples that he was deeply sorrowed, and when he prayed to his Father he asked if there was any way to avoid the suffering that was ahead of him. Jesus had to let go of his fears and prayed, "Yet, not what I want, but what you want." (See *Mark 14:32–36*.)

Scripture

For I am convinced that neither death, nor life, nor angels, nor rulers, nor things present, nor things to come, nor powers, nor height, nor depth, nor anything else in all creation, will be able to separate us from the love of God in Christ Jesus our Lord.
Romans 8:38–39

18th Sunday of Ordinary Time, Cycle A

Skill Steps-

Remember the three steps in managing your emotions: Name it; Tame it; Claim it. Letting go is a matter of saying good-bye to what you are holding on to and saying hello to something new. Remember that every good-bye is followed by a new hello.

Here are some key points to remember:

- The faith of our ancestors in the Old Testament became stronger when they had to let go of the security of what was familiar.
- Jesus, Joseph, Mary, and the apostles all had to practice letting go.
- At times Letting Go may be the most difficult Skill for Christian Living.
- You must learn how to practice letting go in order to avoid worrying about a situation and becoming controlled by an emotion.
- Letting go requires faith that God will bring you to a new hello.
- Taming your reluctance for letting go means that you have to "say good-bye, say hello, and take your time."

Skill Builder-

Read the following situation, and then develop a plan that would help Chris let go.

Share your responses and thoughts with your Faith Partner.

> Chris thinks about Michele all the time. He writes her notes in class and calls her every night. He scribbles her name in his notebooks and watches everything she does. Two weeks ago Michele told Chris that she just wants to be his friend, not his girlfriend.

Name it _____

_____

Tame it _____

_____

Claim it _____

_____

Putting It into Practice-

Pick a situation from your own life where you have not yet been able to let go. Using the skills you developed in *Skill Builder,* work out a tentative plan for yourself.

Name it _____

_____

Tame it _____

_____

Claim it _____

_____

Stress can be a problem for many people. Letting go is a good way to get rid of unnecessary worry and stress.

What do you need to do to improve your ability to let go? Of what in your life do you need to let go?

_____

_____

Closing Prayer-

Lord Jesus, we thank you for showing us what it means to let go of our fears. Help us always respond to your love.

The Holy Spirit

Come, Holy Spirit, and be part of our lives. Fill our hearts with the love of God. Bless us with your presence, and strengthen us so we can respond to God's call.

What Do You Think?

List six one-word Christian qualities. One example might be *honesty.* List your six terms in the spaces below.

_____   _____

_____   _____

_____   _____

If it were suddenly illegal to be a follower of Christ, what evidence might the prosecution present to prove that you were a Christian?

_____

_____

_____

_____

_____

In the Name of the Spirit

Catholics often begin prayers "In the name of the Father, and of the Son, and of the Holy Spirit." In the Old Testament we learn the name of the God of Israel: "I AM WHO I AM" *(Exodus 3:14).* In the New Testament we discover the name of the incarnated Son of God, Jesus. But how do we perceive the Holy Spirit?

There are many titles we use to refer to the Holy Spirit—Comforter, Advocate, Paraclete. But none of them give us a concrete image, like Father or Son. So who is the Holy Spirit in relation to God the Father and God the Son?

We may know the Holy Spirit better than we think. It is through the Holy Spirit that God's grace dwells within us, becomes part of us. Our bodies are said to be temples of the Holy Spirit. (See *1 Corinthians 6:19.*) For instance, think of a time when you were in need of strength or support. You may have prayed. And then perhaps you looked at your problem in a new way. That was the Holy Spirit working within you.

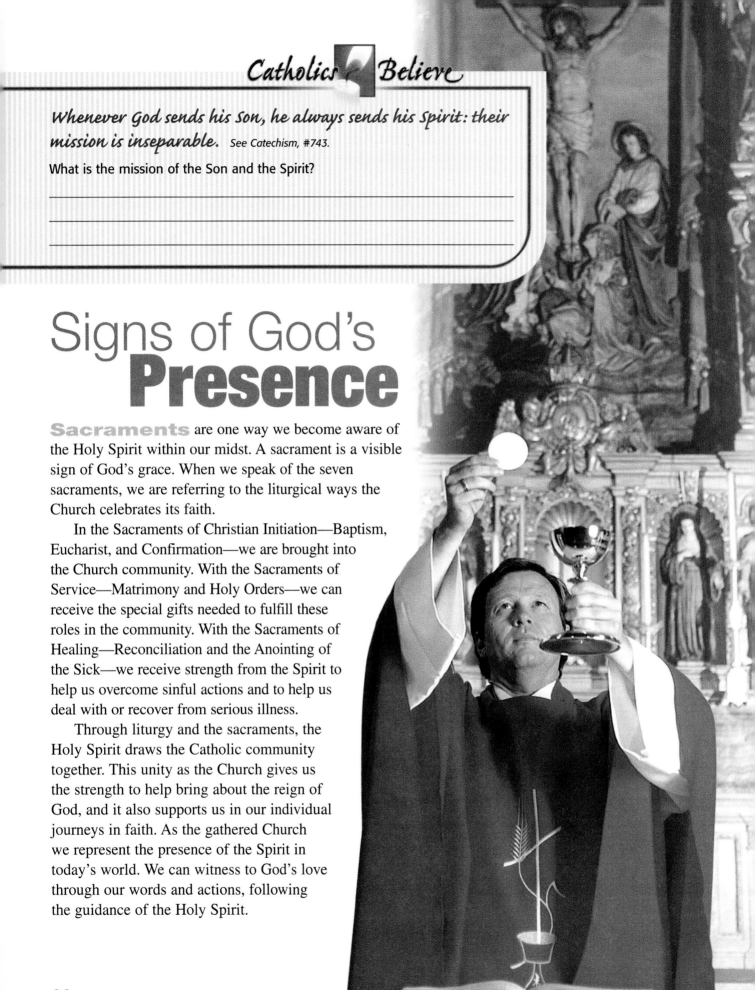

Whenever God sends his Son, he always sends his Spirit: their mission is inseparable. See Catechism, #743.

What is the mission of the Son and the Spirit?

_____

_____

_____

Signs of God's Presence

Sacraments are one way we become aware of the Holy Spirit within our midst. A sacrament is a visible sign of God's grace. When we speak of the seven sacraments, we are referring to the liturgical ways the Church celebrates its faith.

In the Sacraments of Christian Initiation—Baptism, Eucharist, and Confirmation—we are brought into the Church community. With the Sacraments of Service—Matrimony and Holy Orders—we can receive the special gifts needed to fulfill these roles in the community. With the Sacraments of Healing—Reconciliation and the Anointing of the Sick—we receive strength from the Spirit to help us overcome sinful actions and to help us deal with or recover from serious illness.

Through liturgy and the sacraments, the Holy Spirit draws the Catholic community together. This unity as the Church gives us the strength to help bring about the reign of God, and it also supports us in our individual journeys in faith. As the gathered Church we represent the presence of the Spirit in today's world. We can witness to God's love through our words and actions, following the guidance of the Holy Spirit.

Continuing
Strength

Jesus promised his disciples that he would not abandon them. "I will ask the Father, and he will give you another Advocate, to be with you forever" *(John 14:16).*

In Judaism a harvest festival is celebrated each year; it is one of the main Jewish religious festivals. This festival is called **Pentecost,** which in Greek means "the fiftieth day." This celebration is held fifty days after Passover, the commemoration of the Exodus. It was during this festival, when the followers of Jesus were gathered together in prayer, that Jesus' promise to send the Spirit was fulfilled.

In the Acts of the Apostles, which has been called the Gospel of the Holy Spirit, we are told that a noise like a strong, driving wind came from the sky. Then tongues, as of fire, appeared and came to rest upon all of them. All who were present became filled with the Holy Spirit, and from that moment on they began to proclaim the gospel message far and wide. (See *Acts 2:1–4.*)

Promoting Reform

When Angelo Giuseppe Roncalli was elected pope in 1958, he took the name John XXIII. His motto was "In essentials, unity, in doubtful matters, liberty; in all things charity." As pope he was active in promoting social reforms for those whom society overlooked. John XXIII was very interested in ecumenical cooperation with people of other Christian Churches and of other faiths. One year after being elected pope, he called for an ecumenical council to consider the Church in the modern world. This council, known as the Second Vatican Council, considered issues, such as diversity within the Church, the ecumenical movement, and a greater role for lay persons.

Pope John XXIII was also interested in liturgical reform. When he was elected pope, the Mass was said primarily in Latin. He urged the bishops of the world to "open the windows and let the Spirit in." Now the Mass is celebrated most often using the language of the people gathered. Many of Pope John XXIII's other reforms, such as stronger roles for lay people, have also taken hold in the Church. In October 2000 Pope John XXIII was beatified.

For further information: Research to find out other reforms or renewals that Pope John XXIII helped bring about.

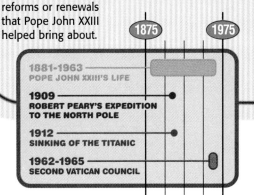

1875

1975

1881-1963
POPE JOHN XXIII'S LIFE

1909
ROBERT PEARY'S EXPEDITION
TO THE NORTH POLE

1912
SINKING OF THE TITANIC

1962-1965
SECOND VATICAN COUNCIL

The Spiritual Life

To be spiritual is to recognize the reality of life beyond the physical world. When we see beyond our possessions and other things that are only of this earth, we come to know real happiness. Think of your own life. You probably have special items given to you by people close to you, such as a stuffed animal that you have had since you were born. As much as you love that item and think that you would never want to lose it, it is the spiritual aspect of the gift that makes it special. Life and the people in your life have the same quality.

All people live in God's presence, and the desire for God is written in the human heart. Christian spirituality is based on a relationship with Christ and on his teachings. This means that we share in Christ's vision of the reign of God and, by our good actions, we are signs of the kingdom.

We know that the reign of God will not be fully realized until the end of time. In the Sermon on the Mount, Jesus reminded people that it is important to go beyond the Ten Commandments. He explained, for example, that it was not enough just to refrain from killing others but that it was important to control anger and become peacemakers, to show mercy to others, and to be humble. The Beatitudes are guidelines for following Christ and helping bring about the reign of God. (See *Matthew 5:1–12.*)

As we face decisions the Holy Spirit is there to assist us with special gifts we call the **gifts of the Holy Spirit.** They are wisdom, understanding, counsel, fortitude, knowledge, piety, and fear of the Lord. We receive these gifts in the Sacrament of Baptism, and they are strengthened in the Sacrament of Confirmation. These gifts help us grow in our relationships with God and others.

Religious communities also receive **charisms,** or divine spiritual gifts. These gifts are given to the individual or to the group of religious in order to help them fulfill their call within the community. The gifts of the Holy Spirit and charisms are ways that our spiritual life is brought into our physical life. By adding more and more spiritual aspects to our life, we gain strength, appreciation, and love. Out of positive acts and choices come positive consequences.

Focus On

The Gifts of the Holy Spirit

Wisdom: using common sense and seeing with the eyes of faith.
Understanding: seeing the relationship between things.
Counsel: exercising right judgment.
Fortitude: courage; knowing what is right and doing the right thing.
Knowledge: distinguishing between truth and falsehood.
Piety: reverence; giving God honor and praise and treating others and all creation with respect.
Fear of the Lord: wonder and awe; responding to God in thanks and praise.

Signs of the **Spirit**

In *Matthew 12:33* Jesus tells his disciples that they can know a tree by its fruit. By the same token, we can know a spiritual person by that person's fruit, or actions. A spiritual person will "bear" the **fruits of the Holy Spirit,** qualities that are signs of the Holy Spirit's presence in a person's life. Paul lists nine of these qualities in his Letter to the Galatians: love, joy, peace, patience, kindness, generosity, gentleness, faithfulness, and self-control. (See *Galatians 5:22–23*.) Some lists of these fruits also include goodness, modesty, and chastity. The Letter to the Colossians adds compassion, humility, meekness, and forgiveness. (See *Colossians 3:12–13*.)

Each of these qualities deals with our relationships with other people. Christian spirituality is always concerned with relationships, both our relationship to other people and our relationship to creation. To grow in Christian spirituality is to be more loving and more joyful in life, to be patient with others and to be aware of the goodness of all creation.

Our experience of the Spirit can be a healing and renewing force. When we live as Christians, we discover that we serve God by serving others.

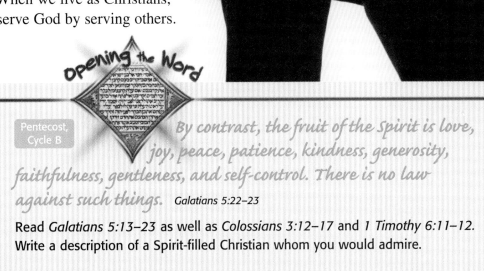

goodness kindness patience generosity joy peace gentleness faithfulness charity self-control chastity modesty

How do you experience the Holy Spirit in your life? Share your responses and thoughts with your Faith Partner.

FAiTH PaRTNeRSHiP

Opening the Word

Pentecost, Cycle B

By contrast, the fruit of the Spirit is love, joy, peace, patience, kindness, generosity, faithfulness, gentleness, and self-control. There is no law against such things. Galatians 5:22–23

Read *Galatians 5:13–23* as well as *Colossians 3:12–17* and *1 Timothy 6:11–12*. Write a description of a Spirit-filled Christian whom you would admire.

_____

_____

Our Own Spirituality

Christian spirituality is not outwardly or even effectively demonstrated by how much we pray or how "in touch" we are with our own faith issues. Instead, our spirituality is best reflected in how we relate to others and how we live our lives. Loving and showing care for others, whether they are close friends or just fellow classmates, illustrates that we acknowledge that God is within all humans.

But no matter how strong our spirituality is, it can always continue to grow and flourish. How can we grow in spiritual ways? There are many personal and communal ways to help us grow in this way. On an individual level we can search for and read new books of prayer or books about the experiences of faith-filled persons. As part of a community, we can grow by attending retreats or by talking with others about faith questions and issues that come up in everyday life.

Like everything else we do in life, spirituality needs to grow. As we mature, we need to allow for the maturing of our faith and the responsibilities that spring from it. The best result of spiritual growth is the serenity and support that comes from deeper understanding of our relationship with God.

Tell how you demonstrate in your life one of the gifts or fruits of the Holy Spirit. Share your thoughts with your Faith Partner.

FaiTH ParTNeRSHiP

WRAP UP

- We come to know the Father and the Son through the Holy Spirit.

- The Holy Spirit is present in the sacraments, our celebrations of faith.

- At the Last Supper Jesus promised to send the Holy Spirit. The promise was fulfilled at Pentecost.

- A Christian spirituality is based in a relationship with Christ and on his teachings.

- Christian spirituality is always concerned with relationships—our relationship to God, to other people, and to creation.

What questions do you have about the information presented in this chapter?

_____

_____

_____

Around the Group

Discuss the following questions as a group.

Suppose that an important decision needs to be made. How do people determine how the Holy Spirit is guiding them? What are the best guidelines to use when making an important decision?

After everyone has had a chance to share his or her responses to the second question, come up with a group answer upon which everyone can agree.

_____

_____

_____

_____

What personal observations do you have about the group discussion and answer?

_____

_____

_____

_____

_____

Briefly...

At the beginning of this chapter, you were asked to list six characteristics of followers of Jesus. How does your list compare with the qualities, or signs of the Holy Spirit's presence, mentioned in the chapter?

_____

_____

_____

Celebrating

Expressions of Faith-

Celebration is an important element of Catholic spirituality. Throughout the history of the Bible, people of God celebrated by writing songs and creating festivals. You, too, are invited to join the people of God who practice celebrating. The trick is doing so in a positive way.

Think About It-

Write about a time when you experienced a good celebration.

_____
_____
_____
_____
_____
_____
_____

Write about a time when you experienced a mediocre celebration.

_____
_____
_____
_____
_____
_____
_____

Skill Steps-

When done properly, celebrating nurtures the spirits of those who join in.

Brainstorm four different occasions that are worth celebrating. Then for each occasion, describe three ways of celebrating—a boring way; a negative way; and a positive, enjoyable way.

1. _____	A) _____
	B) _____
	C) _____
2. _____	A) _____
	B) _____
	C) _____
3. _____	A) _____
	B) _____
	C) _____
4. _____	A) _____
	B) _____
	C) _____

Check It Out-

Place a check mark next to the sentences that apply to you.

○ I enjoy joining in with other people's celebrations.

○ I am creative in coming up with my own ways to celebrate.

○ I am aware of God's presence when I celebrate.

○ My celebrations tend to get out of hand.

○ I am able to find a balance between celebration and other activities.

Based on your responses, what are your strong points and what areas do you need to work on in regard to celebration?

_____

_____

Closing Prayer-

Come, Holy Spirit. Help us be more aware of your presence, and help us find ways to celebrate your presence among us.

CHAPTER

8

A Celebration
of Relationship

Lord Jesus, thank you for the promise of your Spirit sent in your name and for being with us in so many ways. Help us live by your teachings, always growing in our relationship with you.

Rank these relationships in order of the importance they have in your life. (List the responses from 1 to 10, with one being most important and ten being least important.)

_____ Church   _____ music group   _____ sports team

_____ family   _____ scout troop   _____ class or school

_____ friends   _____ youth group   _____ school club

_____ other _____

How does this ranking influence the decisions you make?

_____

_____

_____

A Sense of
Community

Look back at the groups listed in the above activity. Choose one group from the list, other than family, that you ranked of high importance. Are there people within this community whose names you do not know? What different ethnic groups are present in the community? How many different generations participate in this community?

Catholics belong to a very diverse community. Because the Catholic Church is a universal community, members dress in hundreds of different ways, speak thousands of different languages, and quite literally have millions of different ideas about what it means to be Church.

In the early Church it was common to refer to the community of believers as "the saints." After the first centuries it became more common to think of the saints as those members of our community who had already died and were with God. The Church teaches that our community extends beyond death itself, and all of us make up the communion of saints. This means that those who have died in Christ and are in heaven or purgatory, as well as those who are his disciples here on earth together are the communion of saints.

Images of **Church**

We often find it helpful to think in terms of images, or metaphors, when we explore the nature of the Church. In the documents of the Second Vatican Council, the Church was often called the "People of God." This image is borrowed from the Old Testament, where the people of Israel are described as the people of God because of the covenant. The early Christians thought of themselves as having a special relationship with God through the fulfillment of the covenant in Christ and began to think of themselves as people of God.

Another image of the Church is **Body of Christ.** This image views Christ as the head of the Church and the members as the many parts of the body united in him. (See *1 Corinthians 12:12–31.*) The Body of Christ illustrates our unity in faith despite diversity in roles. The image highlights the fact that we must carry out the gospel mission in cooperation with one another according to our own talents.

The Church has also been called the Temple of the Holy Spirit. (See *2 Corinthians 6:16.*) This image highlights the work of the Spirit within the Church through the outpouring of grace. The assembly of believers, united by the Spirit, is strengthened in faith. By expressing charisms, we can renew and build up the Church.

With your Faith Partner, think of a new image, or metaphor, for Church.

FaiTH ParTNeRSHiP

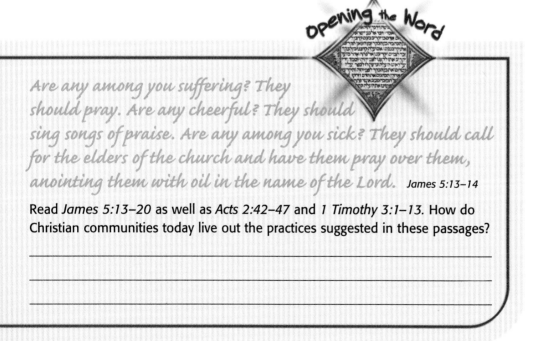

opening the Word

Are any among you suffering? They should pray. Are any cheerful? They should sing songs of praise. Are any among you sick? They should call for the elders of the church and have them pray over them, anointing them with oil in the name of the Lord. James 5:13–14

Read *James 5:13–20* as well as *Acts 2:42–47* and *1 Timothy 3:1–13.* How do Christian communities today live out the practices suggested in these passages?

_____

_____

_____

In a way, these three images reflect our experience of God as Trinity. The Church as the people of God focuses upon the relationship we have with God the Father, especially through covenant. The Church as the Body of Christ focuses upon the relationship we have with Jesus, especially in terms of Christian service. The Church as the Temple of the Holy Spirit focuses on our life in the Spirit, concentrating on the gifts and grace we receive.

The Road to Emmaus

To understand how God reveals himself through the Church, we need to examine one of the appearances of Jesus after he had been raised from the dead.

After Jesus' death two disciples were making their way to the village of Emmaus. They had already heard the report that Jesus' tomb was empty. As they talked about the events of the last few days, Jesus approached and began to walk with them. But the disciples did not recognize him.

When they arrived at Emmaus, it appeared that Jesus was going to continue on, but the disciples, who still did not recognize him, begged him to stay with them. He did so, and when they sat down to dinner he pronounced the blessing, broke the bread, and passed it to them. At this moment they recognized him. (See *Luke 24:13–35*.)

The Church, too, recognizes Jesus in the breaking of the bread. The Eucharist is more than a commemoration of the Last Supper; it is an actual encounter with Jesus. In the Eucharist we participate in the **Paschal mystery,** the mystery of the suffering, death, and resurrection of Jesus.

Our Global Community

The Byzantine Rite

Not all Catholics belong to the Latin Rite of the Church. There are also Eastern Rites, Catholic Churches in union with the Church in Rome who follow different customs, especially in terms of worship. These different Rites evolved through Church history based on the culture of a particular time, place, or people. The largest of these is the Byzantine Rite, which first developed in Constantinople. The Eucharistic liturgy in the Byzantine Rite begins with an elaborate preparation of gifts at a side altar. The priest arranges cubes of leavened bread on the paten in a specific order. After this, litanies are chanted. When the Eucharist is distributed, a golden spoon is used to dip the cubes of Bread into the sacred Wine. Byzantine churches can be identified by the Byzantine cross, which is distinctive in that in addition to the standard crossbar, it includes a lower bar, or foot rest, usually slanted diagonally, and a short upper bar, which represents the inscription *INRI*.

The first purpose of the Church is to be a sacrament, that is, a visible sign of the union between God and people. The Church is also called to be the "sign and instrument" of unity of the human race. *See Catechism, #775.*

How is the Church a sign of unity?

_____

_____

_____

Celebrating
Together

If you could go to a Catholic church in any part of the world, where would you go? What do you imagine it would be like there? In fact, it would be very much like your own church. Liturgy is the public prayer and worship of the Church. The word *liturgy* comes from two Greek words that literally mean "the work of the people." The Eucharistic celebration is the source and summit of Christian life.

Our Eucharistic celebration has two distinct components, both of which are ways we encounter Christ. When we gather together, we tell the story of our faith. This first major part of the Mass is called the **Liturgy of the Word,** which includes the Scripture readings, the homily, the Creed, and general intercessions. It is a celebration of our salvation history, as told in the Scriptures. After that, we begin the **Liturgy of the Eucharist,** which includes the presentation and preparation of the gifts, the Eucharistic Prayer with the consecration of the gifts of bread and wine, and Communion when we receive the sacred Bread and Wine—the Body and Blood of Jesus.

The celebration of the Mass can be said to have two aspects: We gather to tell the story of our faith, and then we break the Bread that unites and sustains us in that faith.

The People of God

"You are a chosen race, a royal priesthood, a holy nation, God's own people, in order that you may proclaim the mighty acts of him who called you out of darkness into his marvelous light" *(1 Peter 2:9)*. As Christians we have been given a mission—to serve, to minister God's word, and to worship God.

To be of service to others, we must take responsibility for our actions and choices. We need to use wise leadership with our friends and siblings, and we should lead lives that mirror Jesus' example, caring for and forgiving others. We can serve others by participating in groups that reach out to those in need, such as in a soup kitchen. But we can also fulfill this royal ministry by listening to someone who needs to talk.

The ministry of God's word, or proclaiming the good news, is our prophetic duty. This ministry involves learning Church teachings, helping others make good choices, and standing up for what we know to be right. We need to let others know about the good news. Sometimes this can even be done through action. A caring act sometimes says more than words.

We can fulfull the priestly ministry to worship God by nurturing our spiritual life, praying, and celebrating the sacraments. Our spirits continually need to be refreshed with God's grace. We can more easily see through a difficult situation if we know that God is within us, providing comfort.

With all the members of the Church performing these ministries, we can truly see that we are the people of God, the sign of his kingdom on earth.

OUR CHRISTIAN JOURNEY

A Doctor of the Church Catherine of Siena apparently began to have mystical experiences at the age of six and experienced visions of Christ, Mary, and some saints. She joined the Third Order of the Dominicans at the age of sixteen. Although she wore the Dominican habit, Catherine was a lay person. She ministered to those who were ill, especially to patients with terminal illnesses.

Later in her life Catherine devoted herself to the cause of unity within the Church. After the election of Pope Urban VI, Catherine worked to bring an end to the Great Schism. She never learned to write, but Catherine dictated her mystical experiences, published under the title *Dialogue,* and many letters. More than four hundred of her letters are still in existence. She died at the age of thirty-three and was made a Doctor of the Church in 1970, the first lay person to be given the title.

For further information: Research Saint Catherine's life in more detail. Focus on what you consider to be her most important service to the Church community.

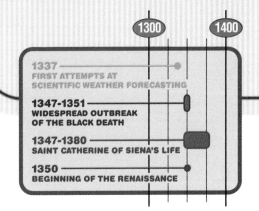

1300   1400

1337
FIRST ATTEMPTS AT
SCIENTIFIC WEATHER FORECASTING

1347-1351
WIDESPREAD OUTBREAK
OF THE BLACK DEATH

1347-1380
SAINT CATHERINE OF SIENA'S LIFE

1350
BEGINNING OF THE RENAISSANCE

Our Celebration

The Mass is not something that we celebrate and then forget about until the next Sunday. We are to take the grace and new understanding that we receive and apply them to the other areas in our lives.

Each gathering at Mass brings us new revelations. Perhaps one Sunday we find comfort; while another Mass brings us knowledge of how to find God in the details of our lives. Whatever the message, it brings us to a closer understanding of God and his reign. We then need to take that message and actually apply what we have learned. Maybe we use the comfort we found to help a friend overcome a particular sadness or frustration. Or we may just need to take time during a busy day to witness God in the details and regain focus on our priorities.

By joining others to celebrate the Liturgy of the Word and the Liturgy of the Eucharist, we not only seek grace and understanding for ourselves, but we recognize that every one of us is in need of those things. We see that we are not alone in our quest for God and his peace. With that realization we can begin to look at others as travelers of the same journey. And perhaps that will help us learn to be patient with others, just as we hope they will be understanding with us. So the Mass is not just about worship, it is also about relationship with God that is then used to strengthen relationships with others.

Reflect on how you celebrate God's presence within the community of believers. Share your thoughts with your Faith Partner.

WRAP UP

- •The Church is a community of believers.

- •Scripture uses three main images to describe the Church: the people of God, the Body of Christ, and the Temple of the Holy Spirit.

- •The Eucharist is an encounter with Jesus.

- •The Church is a sacrament of salvation.

- •The mission of the Church is threefold: service (king), word (prophet), and worship (priest).

What questions do you have about the information presented in this chapter?

_____

_____

_____

Around the Group

Discuss the following question as a group.

Why is communal worship an important part of the Christian life?

After everyone has had a chance to share his or her responses, come up with a group answer upon which everyone can agree.

_____

_____

_____

_____

What personal observations do you have about the group discussion and answer?

_____

_____

_____

_____

Briefly...

What do you see as your role within the Church? What are you able to offer? Look back to _What Do You Think?_ on page 75. Is your rating of your relationship with the Church community the same?

_____

_____

Celebrating

Expressions of Faith-

Celebrating is a characteristic of Catholicism. As Catholics we celebrate with symbols, prayers, feast days, and sacraments.

Skill Steps-

Celebration is one of the major characteristics of Catholicism. Here are some key points to remember:

● Celebrating is a spiritual act. When done properly, it nurtures your spirit and the spirits of others who join in.

● Celebrating, by nature, tends to be communal.

● The Church celebrates through dance, song, music, feasts, festivals, prayers, meals, parties, and liturgy.

● It takes a sense of responsibility to celebrate in healthy ways rather than unhealthy ways.

● Symbols, rituals, prayers, feast days, and sacraments help celebrate friendship with God.

● Catholic ways of celebrating can extend to individual experiences of God.

Skill Builder-

Each of the sacraments has an essential meaning and other related meanings. For each of the four sacraments listed below, the essential meaning of the sacrament is provided. Work with a partner to come up with a related meaning for each sacrament.

Baptism	New life in Christ	_____
Confirmation	An increase in the gifts of the Holy Spirit	_____
Eucharist	Spiritual nourishment	_____
Reconciliation	Forgiveness	_____

Putting It into Practice—

Respond to each question below. Then formulate similar questions based on the *Skill Builder* answers from page 82, and answer those questions.

1. How does your family celebrate new life? _____
2. How do you celebrate receiving a gift? _____
3. What meals do you celebrate in special ways? _____
4. How do you celebrate being forgiven? _____
5. _____? _____
6. _____? _____
7. _____? _____
8. _____? _____

Like all other aspects of our faith, celebrating is a lifelong practice. Be open to new forms of celebration as you experience God's presence in different ways.

What significant moments in young people's lives could be celebrated within the Church community?

_____
_____
_____
_____
_____

Closing Prayer—

Loving God, we celebrate the many ways you have come into our lives. Thank you for including us in the Body of Christ, and help us share the joy of knowing you.

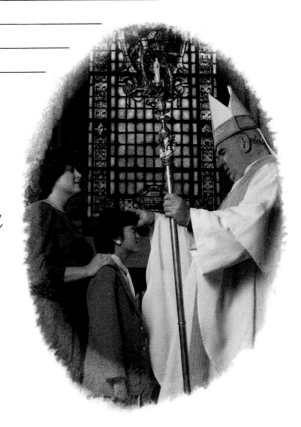

CHAPTER

9

^A Personal Relationship

Lord, teach us to pray. Thank you for your constant readiness to listen to us and for your loving concern. Help us grow closer to you through prayer— speaking, listening, and being in your presence.

Complete the following sentences:

I find it easiest to pray when _____
_____

I find it most difficult to pray when _____
_____

I get the most out of prayer when _____
_____

I feel closest to God when _____
_____

More Than a Wish List

The sound of gunshots echoes in the halls of a high school. During the chaos and violence that follow, many pray for help and survival. Some people lie dead or injured on the floor while others escape to safety.

A mother is diagnosed with terminal cancer. Her family prays fervently for a miracle. The mother dies.

Situations such as these bring us to the mystery of prayer. Our idea of "answered" prayers is challenged. We have to face the fact that a prayer being heard and answered does not necessarily mean getting what we ask for. Instead what prayer sometimes means is that we must offer ourselves and our needs to God and accept his love, even when it is given in ways we do not understand.

"When you are praying, do not heap up empty phrases as the Gentiles do; for they think that they will be heard because of their many words. Do not be like them, for your Father knows what you need before you ask him." Matthew 6:7–8

Read *Matthew 6:5–15* as well as *Matthew 18:19–20* and *Luke 11:9–13*. What do these passages say about prayer?

_____

_____

_____

The Relationship Factor

Think about the importance of communication in any relationship: What sort of relationship would two friends have if they never communicated with each other? Imagine how silly it would be if two friends never spoke with each other, never wrote to each other, never communicated their feelings in any way. The failure to communicate would result in a very empty relationship.

Prayer is our way of relating to God. It is a way of making the relationship grow. We need to take time to listen to how God is calling us. We also need to make ourselves aware of the opportunity to respond to God. Those are the two main activities of prayer: listening and responding. Without prayer a faith life would diminish to nothing more than a set of beliefs.

We do not pray to change God. Rather, prayer is a means of changing ourselves, of helping us participate more actively in the reign of God. This is one way prayer can be seen as affecting the course of human history: that when we pray, we ourselves are changed. The power of prayer is the power of conversion, of changing one's life for the better. Through prayer we constantly grow and change in our faith lives. Prayer is a way of ensuring that our faith does not become stagnant. In prayer we become more and more aware of the presence of the reign of God in our lives.

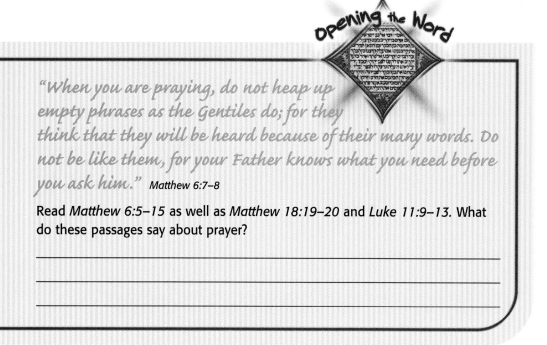

Different Types of Prayer

Prayer can take many different forms and expressions. The Catholic tradition highlights five **forms of prayer** in particular: blessing and adoration, petition, intercession, thanksgiving, and praise. The Eucharist contains and expresses all of these forms of prayer.

Prayers of blessing and adoration help us form a better sense of God's goodness and of the splendor of the reign of God by worshiping our Creator and by recognizing and asking for continued blessings.

In *prayers of petition* we present God with our needs. The request, "give us this day our daily bread," from the Lord's Prayer is an example of petition. We realize, of course, that God is already aware of our needs, but prayers of petition are still appropriate because it is through such prayer that we become aware of our own reliance upon the goodness of God. A prayer of petition is also one way of identifying priorities. Within this form of prayer, we also ask for forgiveness.

Prayers of intercession are prayers presented to God on behalf of others. This form of prayer is rooted in our belief in the communion of saints, to which we all belong. The prayer of intercession is a prayer of unselfish generosity, a way of sharing our concern as a Christian community.

OUR CHRISTIAN JOURNEY

A Life of Prayer

Teresa of Ávila was a member of a contemplative Carmelite community, which had been founded to promote lives of prayer. However, her community was in need of reform, and she was frustrated with the lack of structure and simplicity that she felt was necessary for a life of prayer. Teresa was given permission to organize a reformed community with a stricter, simpler lifestyle. During her lifetime Teresa set up seventeen monasteries for women and sixteen for men, all of which pursued a life of simplicity, poverty, and silence. Teresa had a lively wit and imagination and was known for her sweet temperament. In her book **The Way of Perfection,** she taught that humility is the principal virtue to be practiced by those who pray. Teresa was canonized in 1622 and named a Doctor of the Church in 1970.

For further information: Research to discover how the title Doctor of the Church relates to the works of Saint Teresa of Ávila and Saint Catherine of Siena.

1500   **1575**

c.1500
PORTUGUESE SET UP TRADE
WITH AFRICAN IVORY TRADERS

1515-1582
SAINT TERESA OF ÁVILA'S LIFE

1543
COPERNICUS PUBLISHES
THEORY OF ASTRONOMY

1567
ABDICATION OF
MARY, QUEEN OF SCOTS

Liturgy of the Hours

The Divine Office is an official prayer of the Church. Since 1918 it has been considered the duty of every priest to pray the Office each day. Many men and women religious and lay people also pray the Divine Office. This prayer originated in the fourth century, when a series of nine "hours" were prayed in monasteries and cathedrals. In the thirteenth century these hours were collected into a single volume called a *breviary,* which since the Second Vatican Council has been called the *Liturgy of the Hours.* This volume includes an Office of Readings to be celebrated daily and prayers for specific times of the day, such as *lauds,* or morning prayer, *vespers,* or evening prayer, and *compline,* or night prayer. In the Middle Ages most people could not read. The Rosary developed as a way for those who could not read to pray the hours.

Prayers of thanksgiving characterize the prayers of the Church. For example, the term *eucharist* in Greek means "thanksgiving." Prayers of thanksgiving help us as individuals become aware of how we fit into salvation history. When we thank God for the many gifts we have been given, we come to truly appreciate the grace we have received.

Prayers of praise are prayers that recognize that God is almighty. When we praise God, the Holy Spirit joins with our spirits to bear witness and give glory to the goodness of the reign of God.

Prayer can be expressed in many ways. In **vocal prayer** we express ourselves through words, whether we pray silently or aloud. There are formal, established prayers that we can pray, such as the Lord's Prayer or Saint Francis's Canticle of Praise. Song can also be vocal prayer. But vocal prayer can also be an informal dialogue with God, using our own words.

Meditation is a spiritual exercise that engages the religious imagination. We can begin to meditate by reading Scripture or reflecting on a specific theme, such as how God has been revealed to you during the day. This is followed by dialogue with God.

Contemplative prayer is prayer that takes the form of unspoken dialogue. The point of contemplative prayer is to become aware of God's presence and to unite ourselves with God. A key to contemplation is found in *Psalm 46:10,* "Be still, and know that I am God!" Some of the mystics in Catholic tradition have called this the "Prayer of Quiet." It is thought of as a form of prayer in which a person simply becomes aware of God's goodness. One could think of this sort of prayer as "holy inactivity."

> "Contemplative prayer, in my opinion is nothing else than a close sharing between friends; it means taking time frequently to be alone with him who we know loves us."
>
> *Saint Teresa of Ávila*

Contemplative prayer can happen in the midst of activity and can simply be spending time aware of God's presence. It can take place while walking, jogging, swimming, or cycling. It can happen in a church or in a bathtub. It can be the first activity of the day or the last—any point in the day when a moment can be dedicated to just being with God.

With your Faith Partner, write a short prayer, choosing any form you like. FaiTH PaRTNeRSHiP

Why Pray?

Before it is anything else, prayer is an act of faith. But how do we know that God is listening? We don't, at least not directly, but it is through faith that we encounter God, the One Who Listens. Encountering God through prayer is one of the common elements of all the religions of the world.

The first step in developing a prayer life is realizing why we pray. We pray as a response in grace to the call to conversion; through prayer we can grow, we can change, and we can come to better understand the work of the Holy Spirit in our lives.

One other reason to pray frequently is that God delights in our prayers. Each one of our prayers, no matter its form, is an opportunity for God to "whisper back" how much he loves us.

Catholics Believe

Meditation is a spiritual exercise in which a person seeks to understand the "why and how" of Christian life in order to respond to the Lord's call. See Catechism, #2705.

Using this definition of *meditation*, construct a list of phrases or questions, such as "What has brought me joy today?" that you could use as a starting point for meditation.

_____

_____

_____

The Prayers of Jesus

It is interesting to note how much time Jesus spent in prayer during the years of his active ministry. Immediately after his baptism in the Jordan, Jesus spent forty days in prayer in the desert, preparing himself for his ministry of proclaiming the good news. We are told that Jesus went out to the mountain to pray before selecting his disciples, spending the entire night in communion with God the Father. And he would periodically separate himself from his disciples to pray alone, often walking out into the desert.

Jesus spent a considerable amount of time at prayer in the Garden of Gethsemane the night he was betrayed and tried. And in the Gospel according to Luke, his last act on the cross before he died was a prayer: "Father, into your hands I commend my spirit" *(Luke 23:46)*. With Jesus as our example, we all should be more aware of our own need to communicate with God in prayer.

Life is full of changes, surprises, and sometimes frustration. Whatever forms of prayer you use, God will speak to you, giving you strength, comfort, and understanding. Whether you are having an ongoing quarrel with your best friend or you don't feel that your family understands your emotions, you can always turn to God. When final exams begin and stress hits you or when you vacation at the beach and joy is overwhelming, God is waiting for you to turn to him.

Reflect on the strength of your prayer life. Share your thoughts with your Faith Partner.

FaiTH ParTNeRSHiP

WRAP UP

- Prayer is dialogue with God that deepens our relationship with God by his grace.
- The power of prayer is the power of conversion, of changing one's life for the better by God's grace.
- There are many forms of prayer with many expressions, giving us various ways to listen and respond to God.
- Sometimes prayer is simply being aware of God's presence.

What questions do you have about the information presented in this chapter?

_____

_____

_____

Around the Group

Discuss the following question as a group.

In addition to liturgy, what other ways can you participate in communal prayer?

After everyone has had a chance to share his or her responses, come up with a group answer upon which everyone can agree.

_____

_____

_____

_____

What personal observations do you have about the group discussion and answer?

_____

_____

_____

_____

Briefly...

At the beginning of this chapter, you reflected on prayer in your life. Based on what you have learned about prayer, how can you strengthen your prayer life?

_____

_____

_____

_____

How to Pray

Expressions of Faith—

Just as it takes skill to learn how to communicate with other humans, we need to learn how to communicate with God. By experimenting with various forms of prayer, we can discover levels of spirituality that we didn't know we had. Prayer can be a great source of comfort, hope, guidance, and growth once we learn to overcome distractions.

Think About It—

To assist you in developing the skill of How to Pray, think about how your prayer life has evolved over the course of your life.

○ What are your first memories of prayer?

_____

_____

_____

○ How has your way of praying evolved since you were a child? At what times of day or night do you usually pray?

_____

_____

_____

○ What helps you pray? Music? Pictures or images? Formal prayer? Nature?

_____

_____

_____

Skill Steps-

One of the ways to integrate some of the forms and expressions of prayer is to use the TAPP model:

- **T**hank and praise God for the good things you have been given and the good people in your life.
- **A**dmit the things you may have done wrong or the opportunities to help others that you ignored.
- **P**etition God for your needs and intercede for the needs of others.
- **P**onder what God has to say to you. Practice pausing long enough to listen.

Check It Out-

Circle the responses that best fit your way of praying.

I like

vocal prayer   meditative prayer   memorized prayer   group prayer

I pray

very rarely   once in a while   regularly   often

I listen to God in prayer

rarely   sometimes   always

I thank God in prayer

never   only when things are going well   often

Based on your responses, what are your strong points and what areas do you need to work on?

_____

_____

Closing Prayer-

Thank you, Lord, for hearing our prayers. Forgive us for the times we neglect to turn to you in prayer. Help us hear your voice, and strengthen us in your love.

God's
Presence in Us

Come, Holy

Spirit, make

your presence

known in us.

Fill us with

your gifts so

we might better

serve our

communities.

Guide us in the

fullness of the

reign of God.

Think of three people you know who are good Christians. Then, without writing down anyone's name, list three positive qualities you see in each of the three people you've identified.

Person 1	Person 2	Person 3
_____	_____	_____
_____	_____	_____
_____	_____	_____

A Basic Definition

Who is a Christian? A simple answer might be to say that a Christian is someone who believes in Jesus Christ and responds to his call to "Come, follow me." The invitation comes from God, but the response must come from us.

A Christian is a person who lives that belief and response every day and applies his or her beliefs to every decision. These decisions can be big, such as when a friend wants you to do something that is morally wrong, or small, such as when a family member needs your help and you want to go to a movie instead. A Christian is always a Christian, not just when it is convenient or fun.

"COME FOLLOW ME"

A Life of Power

The word *virtue* comes from the Latin word *virtus,* which means "strength." Virtue provides the strength needed to live a Christian life.

We can actually discover God in the virtues, especially the three **theological virtues:** faith, hope, and love. These gifts from God help us live in relationship with him. *Faith* is the gift of believing in God. Through the virtue of faith we are able to know God and to commit ourselves to being signs of the reign of God. *Hope* in God assists us in developing a vision of possibilities that will carry us through difficulties. *Love,* or charity, is the gift that sends us to love God and others through word and action. Love is faith and hope lived out. According to Paul, it is the greatest of all virtues. (See *1 Corinthians 13:13.*)

The **moral virtues** deal with how we relate to other people. These habits are prudence, justice, temperance, and fortitude. Many people refer to these as the cardinal virtues because all the other habits of goodness depend on these four virtues.

Prudence guides our conscience and keeps us from acting thoughtlessly or foolishly. *Temperance* is the virtue of moderation. It helps us balance our wants and needs, curbing selfishness and materialism. *Fortitude* gives us moral courage, allowing us to do what is right even when it may not be easy to do so.

Justice is the virtue that helps us give to God and to others what is due them. Justice requires that we acknowledge God and worship him. When it comes to our relationships with other people, justice is concern for rights and duties. A right is a person's moral claim upon society, such as the right to food. Duties flow from rights.

Opening the Word

5th Sunday of Easter, Cycle B

And this is his commandment, that we should believe in the name of his Son Jesus Christ and love one another, just as he has commanded us. All who obey his commandments abide in him, and he abides in them. And by this we know that he abides in us, by the spirit that he has given us. 1 John 3:23–24

Read *1 John 3:17–24* as well as *Matthew 5:43–48, Mark 12:28–34,* and *1 John 4:7–18.* What is meant by loving in deed and truth?

_____

_____

For example, our duty to care for the environment comes from everyone's right to clean water and air. When people are irresponsible or worse, justice becomes a factor. It helps us regulate our relationships. When we love others unselfishly, justice is realized.

Justice has three basic forms. Commutative justice regulates the relationships between persons and between persons and institutions. *Commutative* means "to exchange or to replace." An example of commutative justice is paying our financial debts. Distributive justice regulates what the community owes its members in proportion to their contributions and needs. *Distributive* is derived from the term *distribution*. The federal law that sets a minimum wage for workers is distributive justice. Legal justice is concerned with what the individual in fairness owes the community. Community regulations covering things such as littering help members act fairly, respecting the rights of others.

As Christians we are called to perform works for the common good, or works that will benefit the entire community. There are three essential elements necessary for the common good. The first element is respect for each person. This respect is due each person because of his or her human **dignity,** which comes from having been created in God's image. The second aspect is the social well being or development of the entire group. Things such as education, health care, and culture should be accessible to all members, allowing them to lead a truly human life— not just to survive. The final element is peace. This is the role of the state, which has the duty to protect its members.

With the help of God's grace, we can nurture the moral virtues with education, chosen and repeated acts, and determination. We can become more and more virtuous as we go through our lives.

Focus On

Social Justice
Social justice means giving each person his or her due, regardless of education, race, gender, or background, because each person is a child of God. Working toward the promotion of justice and the common good is not just something we do to be kind and loving to others. Rather, it is preaching the gospel through actions. The Church's mission is to preserve and promote the common good for all members of the human race against all forms of oppression.

The Heart of All Virtues

Every virtue is an expression of love, both in terms of the love we have for God and our love of neighbor. Virtue is inspired by love. For example, without love, fortitude is nothing more than recklessness. Temperance, without love, would be nothing more than cautiousness. Without love, justice becomes a strict application of rules. Prudence, without love, leads to safe decisions based on self-interest.

Followers of Jesus are challenged to live out these human virtues and others, such as mercy, honesty, compassion, perseverance, reverence, faithfulness, and loyalty. In some form or another, these virtues are all inspired by love.

Virtue and action go hand in hand. Mercy, for example, goes beyond compassion and good wishes. Works of mercy, such as feeding the hungry and comforting the grieving, are an important part of the life of virtue. Because we are aware of the worth and nobility of the human person, we are led to perform works of mercy.

Our Christian Journey

Helping Out Since 1956 more than seven thousand volunteers have dedicated one year of service after graduation from college to the Jesuit Volunteer Corps. The volunteers put off graduate school or career opportunities in order to work with those in need. The goal of the Jesuit Volunteer Corps is to provide alternatives to people who have few options. The corps helps those who are unemployed, homeless, elderly, infected with AIDS, troubled, abused, mentally ill, or developmentally disabled.

The Franciscans, the Benedictines, and the Salesians also lead volunteer organizations. The Holy Cross Associates, the Christian Brothers Volunteers, the Augustinian Volunteer Program, and the Franciscan Workers of Junipero Serra are other examples. A directory of such organizations has been put together by the Catholic Network of Volunteer Service and is available on the Internet.

For further information: Check out the Web site of the Catholic Network of Volunteer Service at **www.cnvs.org.** Is there an organization close to where you live? Which one appeals to you?

Catholics Believe

Social justice can be obtained only when the dignity of all people is respected. The promotion of human dignity is entrusted to us by God. *See Catechism, #1929.*

What are ways human dignity can be promoted by society?

_____

_____

Responding to the Call

The Christian life is also a life of **discipleship.** Discipleship is a way of life for those who follow Jesus and spread the good news of God's saving love.

Answering the call to discipleship in the days of Jesus was not a casual matter. Jesus invited people to leave their homes, their careers, and even their families in order to follow him. He advised one rich young man that, before becoming a disciple, he should sell all that he had and give the money to those in need.

All Christians share the call of discipleship. Each of us is called to share our faith through how we live our lives. We are called to **witness** to our faith, sharing the good news by living a life of virtue.

Jesus told his disciples that they were the light of the world. (See *Matthew 5:14–16.*) He reminded them of how unusual it would be to light a lamp but hide it under a bushel basket. Instead the lamp should be on a stand where it can give light to the whole house. In the same way, Jesus asked his disciples to let their light shine before all people so the goodness in their acts could be seen.

In the modern Church working for justice is a major responsibility. It is not a choice; the only choice is *how* we will work for justice. As Christians we need to be deeply committed to the promotion of the dignity of all people.

With your Faith Partner, discuss why working for justice is not an option but a requirement for Christians.

FaiTH PaRTNeRSHiP

Christian Witness

Words alone are not as powerful as words backed up by actions.

The Catholic approach to sharing our faith has generally been that of Peter, who in his first letter says that if anyone should ask the reason for our hope, we should be ready to reply, but we should speak gently and reverently. (See *1 Peter 3:15–16*.)

Why would anyone ask about the reason we are such hopeful people? Because they've read our bumper stickers? No. They would ask because they have seen our strength of character, and they want to know the reason for our hope.

The best way to communicate the gospel is to live it. We can spread the love of God by responding lovingly to the needs of other people. Our faith revolves around the principle that we serve God best by serving other people.

The disciples learned many lessons from Jesus during the three years of his public ministry, but one of the most important was the lesson he taught them on the night he was betrayed. During their last meal together, Jesus washed the feet of each of his disciples. This was a task for the lowliest of servants. And yet, this is the model that Jesus wanted his disciples to adopt, that of servants.

Reflect on how we can be witnesses to God every day. Share your thoughts with your Faith Partner.

FaiTH PaRTNeRSHiP

WRAP UP

• A virtue is a strength rooted in grace.

• The theological virtues help us live in relationship with God.

• The moral virtues deal with how we relate to other people.

• Virtue becomes the means through which we accomplish moral good.

• All Christians are called to discipleship and to be witnesses to our faith.

Write down any questions you have about the information presented in this chapter.

_____

_____

_____

Around the Group

Discuss the following question as a group.

How does the call to discipleship apply to people your age?

After everyone has had a chance to share his or her responses, come up with a group answer upon which everyone can agree.

_____

_____

_____

_____

What personal observations do you have about the group discussion and answer?

_____

_____

_____

_____

_____

Briefly...

At the beginning of this chapter, you were asked to list qualities you admire in people you know. How do the qualities you listed compare with the moral and theological virtues?

_____

_____

_____

How to Pray

Expressions of Faith—

Prayer is a two-way communication with God and should therefore involve as much listening as it does talking. To help with the listening element of prayer, we need to develop the prayer of quiet, that component of prayer that does not rely on language.

Skill Steps—

There is a difference between learning about prayer and learning how to pray. Learning how to pray requires discipline.
   Here are some key points to remember:

● You can **TAPP** into God's presence through the four steps: **Thank, Admit, Petition,** and **Ponder.**

● When you **TAPP** into God's presence, your prayer life can improve, and it makes it more difficult to be distracted.

● Sometimes you can pray better through experiences than with words.

● Pray often and everywhere. That is the secret to developing your own real and strong spirituality.

Skill Builder—

Below are possible situations in which you might pray. Put one of the following symbols in the space preceding each possibility: ✗ = would not work for you, ★ = works for you, ✔ = would like to try, ? = not certain.

_____ While listening to music   _____ While hiking

_____ While running or jogging   _____ While sitting alone in a church

_____ While bathing   _____ While eating lunch alone

_____ While traveling in a car or bus   _____ While waiting in line

_____ While observing nature   _____ While writing in a journal

See if you can find any pattern in your responses.

_____

Putting It into Practice—

Some people find that keeping a prayer list organizes their prayer lives. Construct a list of things for which you wish to pray.

● **Thank:** List three things for which you want to thank or praise God.

_____

_____

_____

● **Admit:** List three areas of your life in which you want to grow in holiness.

_____

_____

_____

● **Petition and intercession:** List three needs for yourself or others for which you want to pray.

_____

_____

_____

● **Ponder:** List three ways you can practice pausing to listen to what God has to say to you.

_____

_____

_____

Remember to be honest when you pray. God knows your fears and your needs. By reflecting on your prayer needs, you can help yourself find ways to deal with your needs and the needs of others.

Which area of your prayer life do you need to improve?

_____

_____

Closing Prayer—

Holy Spirit, remain in my heart as I encounter the many surprises, difficulties, and joys of life. Guide me to turn to God in prayer for gratitude, comfort, and sharing happiness. Amen.

Prayers and **Resources**

The Lord's Prayer

Our Father, who art in heaven,
hallowed be thy name;
thy kingdom come;
thy will be done on earth as it is in heaven.
Give us this day our daily bread;
and forgive us our trespasses
as we forgive those who trespass against us;
and lead us not into temptation,
but deliver us from evil.
Amen.

Hail Mary

Hail, Mary, full of grace,
the Lord is with you!
Blessed are you among women,
and blessed is the fruit of your womb, Jesus.
Holy Mary, Mother of God,
pray for us sinners,
now and at the hour of our death.
Amen.

THE TEN COMMANDMENTS

1. I am the Lord your God. You shall not have strange gods before me.

2. You shall not take the name of the Lord your God in vain.

3. Remember to keep holy the Lord's day.

4. Honor your father and your mother.

5. You shall not kill.

6. You shall not commit adultery.

7. You shall not steal.

8. You shall not bear false witness against your neighbor.

9. You shall not covet your neighbor's wife.

10. You shall not covet your neighbor's goods.

Resources

THE BEATITUDES

Blessed are the poor in spirit,
  for theirs is the kingdom
    of heaven.

Blessed are they who mourn,
  for they will be comforted.

Blessed are the meek,
  for they will inherit the land.

Blessed are they who hunger and
thirst for righteousness,
  for they will be satisfied.

Blessed are the merciful,
  for they will be shown mercy.

Blessed are the clean of heart,
  for they will see God.

Blessed are the peacemakers,
  for they will be called children
    of God.

Blessed are they who are persecuted
for the sake of righteousness,
  for theirs is the kingdom
    of heaven.

(Matthew 5:3–10)

Glory to the Father (Doxology)

Glory to the Father, and to the Son,
and to the Holy Spirit:
as it was in the beginning, is now,
and will be for ever.
Amen.

Gifts of the Holy Spirit

Wisdom
Understanding
Right judgment (Counsel)
Courage (Fortitude)
Knowledge
Reverence (Piety)
Wonder and awe (Fear of the Lord)

Fruits of the Spirit

Charity
Joy
Peace
Patience
Kindness
Goodness
Generosity
Gentleness
Faithfulness
Modesty
Self-control
Chastity

Act of Contrition

My God,
I am sorry for my sins with all my
heart.
In choosing to do wrong
and failing to do good,
I have sinned against you
whom I should love above all things.
I firmly intend, with your help,
to do penance,
to sin no more,
and to avoid whatever leads me to sin.
Our Savior Jesus Christ
suffered and died for us.
In his name, my God, have mercy.

Works of Mercy

Corporal (for the body)
Feed the hungry.
Give drink to the thirsty.
Clothe the naked.
Shelter the homeless.
Visit the sick.
Visit the imprisoned.
Bury the dead.

Spiritual (for the spirit)
Warn the sinner.
Teach the ignorant.
Counsel the doubtful.
Comfort the sorrowful.
Bear wrongs patiently.
Forgive injuries.
Pray for the living and the dead.

PRECEPTS OF THE CHURCH

1. Take part in the Mass on
   Sundays and holy days. Keep
   these days holy and avoid
   unnecessary work.

2. Celebrate the Sacrament of
   Reconciliation at least once
   a year if there is serious sin.

3. Receive Holy Communion at
   least once a year during
   Easter time.

4. Fast and abstain on days
   of penance.

5. Give your time, gifts, and
   money to support the Church.

The Apostles' Creed

I believe in God, the Father almighty,
  creator of heaven and earth.
I believe in Jesus Christ, his only Son,
  our Lord.
  He was conceived by the power of the
  Holy Spirit
  and born of the Virgin Mary.
  He suffered under Pontius Pilate,
  was crucified, died, and was buried.
  He descended to the dead.
  On the third day, he rose again.

He ascended into heaven,
  and is seated at the right hand
  of the Father.
  He will come again to judge the
  living and the dead.
I believe in the Holy Spirit,
  the holy catholic Church,
  the communion of saints,
  the forgiveness of sins,
  the resurrection of the body,
  and life everlasting. Amen.

The Nicene Creed

We believe in one God,
  the Father, the Almighty,
  maker of heaven and earth,
  of all that is, seen and unseen.
We believe in one Lord, Jesus Christ,
  the only Son of God,
  eternally begotten of the Father,
  God from God, Light from Light,
  true God from true God,
  begotten, not made, one in Being
  with the Father.
  Through him all things were made.
  For us men and for our salvation
  he came down from heaven:
  by the power of the Holy Spirit
  he was born of the Virgin Mary,
  and became man.
  For our sake he was crucified under
  Pontius Pilate;
  he suffered, died, and was buried.
  On the third day he rose again
  in fulfillment of the Scriptures;

he ascended into heaven
  and is seated at the right hand
  of the Father.
  He will come again in glory to judge
  the living and the dead,
  and his kingdom will have no end.
We believe in the Holy Spirit, the Lord,
  the giver of life,
  who proceeds from the Father and
  the Son.
  With the Father and the Son he is
  worshiped and glorified.
  He has spoken through the Prophets.
We believe in one holy catholic and
  apostolic Church.
We acknowledge one baptism for the
  forgiveness of sins.
We look for the resurrection
  of the dead,
  and the life of the world to come.
  Amen.

The Liturgical Year

In the liturgical year the Church celebrates Jesus' life, death, resurrection, and ascension through its seasons and holy days. The liturgical year begins with the First Sunday of Advent.

The readings for the entire Church year are contained in the Lectionary. Readings for Sundays and solemnities of the Lord are placed in a three-year rotation—Cycle A, Cycle B, and Cycle C.

The Season of Advent begins in late November or early December. During Advent we recall the first coming of the Son of God into human history, and we prepare for the coming of Christ—in our hearts, in history, and at the end of time. The liturgical color for Advent is violet.

On Christmas we celebrate the Incarnation, the Son of God becoming one of us. The color for Christmas is white, a symbol of celebration and life in Christ. (Any time white is used, gold may be used.)

Lent is the season of prayer and sacrifice that begins with Ash Wednesday and lasts about forty days. Lent has always been a time of repentance through prayer, fasting, and almsgiving. The liturgical color for Lent is purple, a symbol of penance.

Easter is the high point of the liturgical year because it celebrates Jesus' resurrection from the dead. The week beginning with Palm Sunday is called Holy Week. Lent ends on Holy Thursday evening, when the Easter Triduum begins. The Triduum, or "three holy days," includes the observance of Holy Thursday, Good Friday, and the Easter Vigil on Holy Saturday. The liturgical color for the Easter Season is white, a symbol of our joy in experiencing new life in Christ. The Easter Season lasts about seven weeks (fifty days).

At Pentecost, we celebrate the gift of the Holy Spirit sent to the followers of Jesus gathered in the upper room in Jerusalem. The liturgical color for Pentecost is red, a symbol of the tongues as of fire on Pentecost and of how Christ and some of his followers (such as the early Christian martyrs) sacrificed their lives for love of God.

The majority of the liturgical year is called Ordinary Time, a time when the Church community reflects on what it means to walk in the footsteps of Jesus. The liturgical color for Ordinary Time is green, a symbol of hope and growth.

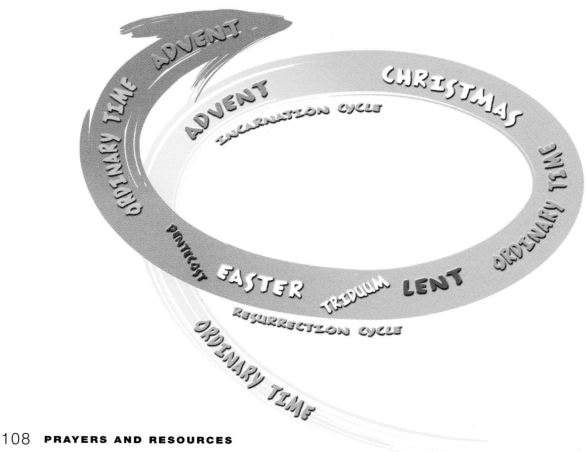

Glossary

A annunciation — The announcement to Mary that she would conceive by the Holy Spirit a baby, the Son of God.

B Body of Christ — The Church; Christ is the head of the Body, and we as baptized members are united with one another; each of us has a function to perform as part of the Church.

C charism — A divine spiritual gift given by the Holy Spirit to individuals or groups for the good of the community.

contemplative prayer — Prayer of communion with God in an unspoken dialogue.

covenant — A sacred and binding promise or agreement joining God and humans in relationship. Jesus' sacrifice established the new and everlasting covenant, open to all who do God's will.

D Decalogue — The Ten Commandments; God's laws given to the Hebrew people as part of the covenant at Sinai.

dignity — The respect due to every human that comes from our having been created in God's image.

discipleship — A way of life for those who follow Jesus and spread the good news of God's saving love.

E Exodus — The Hebrew people's journey from slavery in Egypt to freedom in the promised land, directed and accomplished by God.

F faith — The gift given to us by God that moves us to seek him out and believe in him.

fiat — Mary's answer to the angel, offering herself to God at the annunciation.

forms of prayer — Basic ways we respond to and deepen our relationship with God: blessing and adoration, petition, intercession, thanksgiving, and praise.

fruits of the Holy Spirit — Qualities that are signs of the Holy Spirit's presence. The twelve fruits are charity, joy, peace, patience, kindness, goodness, generosity, gentleness, faithfulness, modesty, self-control, and chastity.

G gifts of the Holy Spirit — The seven powerful gifts received in Baptism and strengthened in Confirmation that help us grow in our relationships with God and with others. The seven gifts are wisdom, understanding, counsel (right judgment), fortitude (courage), knowledge, piety (reverence), and fear of the Lord (wonder and awe).

grace — God's life in us through the Holy Spirit, freely given; our loving relationship with God; the free and undeserved help God gives us so that we may respond to the call to holiness.

H Holy Trinity — One God in three Persons—Father, Son, and Holy Spirit. The Trinity is the central mystery of the Catholic faith.

I incarnation — God the Son's becoming human in Jesus.

inspiration — Guidance from the Holy Spirit in the writing and the formation of Scripture.

interdependence — People relying on each other and being responsible for one another.

J justice — The moral virtue that helps us give to God and others what is due them.

L Liturgy of the Eucharist — The term for the entire celebration of the Mass as well as for the specific part of the Mass that includes the Preparation of the Gifts, the Eucharistic Prayer, and Communion.

Liturgy of the Word — The first great part of the Mass, lasting from the first reading to the General Intercessions, that celebrates God's word.

M Magnificat — The Canticle of Mary; Mary's song of praise to the Lord.

meditation — Prayer that engages thought, imagination, emotion, and desire to bring a person to God and to deepen the Christian life.

moral virtues — The firm attitudes and habits that help us live in relationship with God and with each other—prudence, justice, temperance, and fortitude.

mystery — A truth of our faith that we cannot fully understand but that we believe because God has revealed it.

P Paschal mystery — The saving mystery of Jesus' passion, death, resurrection, and ascension.

Pentecost — The descent of the Holy Spirit upon the apostles fifty days after Easter. The word *Pentecost* means "the fiftieth day."

providence — God's protection and governance over all things.

R religion — A system of beliefs, worship, and tradition that helps us express our faith in God.

revelation — The process by which God makes himself known to us. The chief sources of revelation are God's creation, Scripture, salvation history, and Jesus (the fullness of revelation).

S sacrament — A celebration in which Jesus joins with the assembled community in liturgical actions that are efficacious signs and sources of God's grace.

salvation history — The story of God's loving actions on behalf of humans. Salvation history began with creation, continues through the events recorded in Scripture, and will last until the end of time.

stewardship — Responsible care for creation.

T theological virtues — The three great gifts from God that help us live in relationship with him—faith, hope, and love.

V vocal prayer — Prayer that is expressed in words, which may be our own words or the words of others.

W witness — Sharing one's beliefs and values in words and actions.

Index